INSPIRE LOVE

Inspiring Stories of God's Love
for and between His Children

Dear Janice,
Thank you for
your love, support,
encouragement, prayers
and friendship.
Thank you for you!

INSPIRE LOVE

**Inspiring Stories of God's Love
for and between His Children**

Edited by Michelle Janene & Dana Sudboro

INSPIRE PRESS
Sacramento, CA

ISBN-13: 978-1-938196-12-6

Inspire Press, PO Box 276794, Sacramento, CA 95827, USA
http://inspirewriters.com

Cover photo by Josh Willink from Pexels / Image ID : 286625

Printed in United States of America

STAR WARS, BABY DOLLS, AND HOLDING HANDS

Rosemary Johnson

At times, empathy is overrated. Sometimes it feels like I have a superpower—able to sponge up everyone's feelings, especially those I care about. Other times, I'm too lost in my own head to even notice what's going on. But when I do pay attention, it hurts.

As a caregiver at a senior living facility, I mostly work in memory care. Lots of nights, I dream that I'm trapped at work and can't figure out where I am. Usually, I wake up screaming on those nights. Once, I woke, standing by my bed, pounding on the wall. Maybe it's because on some level, every single one of our fifteen residents knows they are trapped behind the alarmed doors, and I feel it, too.

There are days where I feel like I'm the one who is losing my mind. Days where the physically fit male resident follows me around, standing within two feet of me, and I'm terrified he'll start acting like I'm his girlfriend again, or I'll say the wrong thing and he'll get mad and hit me. Or days where I'm cleaning up poop and vomit and giving extra showers.

At one point, my knuckles cracked from washing my hands so much and taking vinyl gloves off and on all day.

Some days, I have to lie. They all live in their own worlds, and when a woman asks where is her family, I can't tell her that her husband never visits and her children live far away. I have to say, "They'll be here soon, maybe after dinner." She usually asks for them several times, every evening. It's always worse when the sun goes down. She knows the words to just about every old song there is, though, and can spell "antidisestablishmentarianism" without pausing.

One resident is on Hospice and hardly ever leaves her room, but I always blow her a kiss when I leave. Her face lights up, and she'll blow a kiss back, very slowly, because fast for her leaves a snail seeming like it has a cheetah's speed. Once, I pretended to catch her kiss and put it in my apron pocket. She laughed out loud.

Another resident has aphasia. She understands everything you say and will chatter and chatter, but her words sound like one long stutter. Sometimes I can understand, or at least understand enough to get the gist of what she's saying. It's the best when she tells me a story, flinging her hands around, making sound effects, and ending with a laugh and a hug. She gives the best hugs. She also keeps things organized and can spot a speck of dirt on the floor from across the room.

I'm always careful when I turn down her bed, because when the sheets are wrinkled, she has to fix them before she climbs in. As another person with OCD traits, I get it. Anyway, I have an odd liking for making beds.

One night after everyone was in bed, my fellow geek coworker and I put on the movie, *Star Wars: The Force Awakens*. Our night owl resident came in with her walker and sat next to me, completely engrossed. During a desert scene, she leaned toward me and whispered, "Are they on the prairie?"

I told her, "No, they're on another planet in another galaxy. It's science fiction."

"No kidding!" She gasped and scooted forward, focusing with twice the rapt attention.

I've been told things like, "You're just full of beans," or "It's better when you're here," and the one that made me laugh, "You're so beautiful for a boy." Maybe it's because I wear my waist-length hair in a bun for work and my uniform looks like an officer's uniform with its dark colors and the *walkie and earpiece I wear.*

The French resident doesn't speak English much anymore. She likes to come into the activity room after everyone is in bed, cradling her baby doll, and tell me all sorts of things I can't understand. But when I say "Good night, see you tomorrow!" in French, she grins and the skin around her eyes crinkles like a walnut shell.

There is a pianist who enjoys playing on the upright piano in the dining room, muttering, "Okay, okay, okay," the whole time she plays. Sometimes she follows the sheet music, but most of the time she makes it up.

The French lady will come in and dance, clicking her tongue in rhythm, swishing her skirt like a flirting schoolgirl.

Occasionally a harpist will come and play for us, and our resident soprano opera singer will sing along. Her voice is still lovely. Her room smells like dried flowers, and she always dresses elegantly.

Talking to them and seeing their rooms, their mannerisms, it's like looking at ghosts from their past. What operas did the soprano sing? What atrocities did the French woman witness in WWII? And why does another woman hoard folded bits of toilet paper?

The worst is when they cry. My pint-sized resident, who likes to shuffle along beside me holding my hand, sometimes cries because she's lonely. All I can do is sit with her, my arm around her shoulders.

Except…maybe that's exactly what she needs. Because when I leave, she's smiling. When I get her ready for bed, I whisper, "I love you," and mean it. She says it back and asks if I'm coming back tomorrow. My answer is usually, "Yes." And then, when I do walk into the activity room the next day and pat her on the hand, she grins and says, "That's right." If my hands are cold, which they usually are, she'll cover them with her swollen fingers until they're warm.

Maybe empathy isn't overrated. I know one thing, though—love certainly isn't.

Rosemary E. Johnson lives in the beautiful Sierra-Nevada mountain foothills. She is known to carry on conversations with her cat, make fairy houses, and run around barefoot. She has three short stories published in anthologies by Inspire Press, and one with The Crossover Alliance.

LOVE MOVED THE MOUNTAIN

Lois Loofbourrow

I met Mai Tang several years ago. As my manicurist, she shared bits and pieces of her difficult childhood during the Vietnam War. Her little brother died and was buried in her uncle's backyard. Mai held her beloved father, as he gasped his last breath. After the war, the Viet Cong rationed food, water, and electricity, not according to family members, but per house—someone always went hungry. Her stories were captivating.

The Lord placed a burden on my heart, and I prayed, *Lord, how can I reach Mai for You? She has shared some painful childhood memories. She is Buddhist, and I want to tell her how much You love her, no matter what has happened in her life.*

The Lord spoke softly to my heart, *Write her story. Leave the rest to Me.*

But Lord, I work forty hours a week, attend Bible College, and teach Sunday School. I do love to write, and even belong to Inspire Christian Writers, but I just don't have the time.

He patiently repeated, *Write her story. Leave the rest to Me.* I surrendered and simply said, "Yes, Lord."

On my way to see Mai for my next appointment, I thought, *Maybe she won't want to share her personal life…some things are best left unspoken.* As Mai began to buff my nails, I took a leap of faith and asked, "Mai, can I write about your life in Vietnam?"

She stopped, let go of my hand, and looked straight into my eyes and asked, "You want to write my story? Will it be a book? Yes! When do we begin?"

Over the course of the next three years, Mai talked about her life in Vietnam. As she filed and polished my nails, I wrote with my right hand, and then the left—a feat in and of itself. I asked personal questions and she answered to the best of her memory. Her first job, at the age of eight, was taking care of three small children, six days a week, eight hours a day. Mai shared of betrayal and rejection by her mother. The tears flowed, recalling memories of molestation and standing silent in the face of abuse. Then she spoke of a deepest pain— attempted suicide.

I was shocked. I had no idea of the depths of her suffering. But Jesus knew. His love for Mai reached back to her childhood, calling her to Him.

As I undertook this project, I realized I had to grow as a writer. The Lord stretched me as I diligently worked on Mai's manuscript. I would edit my bi-monthly scribble, submit the chapters to my writer's group, and most importantly—pray for Mai's salvation. Then I would read each draft to Mai for her approval.

As we were almost finished with the book, her son tragically took his life. It seemed like Mai's world in America was falling apart. I sensed in my spirit, it was not appropriate to continue our work. When I sat down for my next appointment, I said, "Mai, maybe we need to stop writing for now. Do you want me to pray for you?"

She nodded, as tears flowed from the deep anguish of a broken heart. I gently took her hands and prayed, "Dear Jesus, please hold Mai. Let her feel Your love during this difficult time. Hold her family in Your loving arms."

After I left, my heart was breaking. *Lord, I feel so helpless. What can I do?*

The Lord whispered, *Pray. Pray for Mai and her family. Leave the rest to Me.*

❧

A couple of months later, Mai said, "Lois, I'd like to try to finish the book."

Surprised, I hesitated. "Are you sure? Mai, the rest of your family does not know about the molestations and attempted suicide. Will this be too much?"

She took a deep breath and said, "My family needs to know. My son was depressed, and in my culture, we keep those things a secret. We're supposed to be silent about our hidden pain. Also, for the last couple of years, everyone in the shop has watched us work on the book, and my customers keep asking when it will be done?"

And so, we completed *Silent Obedience, Mai's Story, a Vietnam Memoir of Endurance and Hope,* and dedicated the book to her son. It was a best seller at her shop.

Although the book was a success, Mai and her husband, Mr. Tang, continued to grieve the loss of their son. A caring customer gave Mai a Catholic prayer book, and though she didn't understand the words it gave her some comfort. I arrived at one appointment and found Mai weeping. "Lois, I miss my son so much. I don't know what to do. I feel so empty when I go to the Buddhist temple with my family."

I felt the Lord's nudge and said, "Mai, do you want me to pray for you? Do you want to ask Jesus into your heart?"

She nodded, bowed her head and said, "Yes."

Tears rolled down my face, as I witnessed the humble opening of a child-like heart to Jesus. This was the reason; this was the moment in eternity for Mai's story. I reached for her hands and together we said the sinner's prayer. All of heaven rejoiced as Mai accepted the love of Jesus into her heart.

"Mai, you are now in the family of God, a precious child of our loving Heavenly Father. Now, we need to find you a Vietnamese church."

"Ok, you find the church, but you'll need to take me, since I don't drive. I hope Mr. Tang lets me go to a Christian church. I'll have to ask…"

The next Sunday, Mr. Tang allowed me to pick up Mai, and we drove to a local Vietnamese church. Mai listened to the sermon in Vietnamese, as I wore headphones.

After the church service, the Lord seemed to whisper again, *Pray for Mr. Tang. Leave the rest to Me.*

As we drove away, I said, "Mai, we need to pray for Mr. Tang. Jesus loves him as much as He loves us."

"Oh no, he's a strong Buddhist. I can't talk to him about Jesus. I'm just thankful he lets me go to church."

"But Mai, it says in the Bible, if we pray, God will move mountains. Only God's love can humble the heart…"

"Ok, you pray, because Mr. Tang is a really big mountain!"

☙

Mai and her family relocated to the other side of town. I could no longer drive her to church, but Mr. Tang, surprisingly, offered to take her. He would sit in the church parking lot and wait until the service ended.

At our next appointment, Mai smiled and said, "The mountain has moved!"

I lifted my hands in praise, "Thank you Jesus! Tell me what happened?"

"I found another Vietnamese church that I like. One of the church elders came out to speak with Mr. Tang in the parking lot. I was shocked when I saw him walk inside the church with the elder, and even more so when he sat down next to me. My heart was pounding. I didn't say a word, just thanked Jesus in my heart. After the service, I told my husband, whatever you do, whatever you decide, just do it from your heart."

The church elder and his wife welcomed Mai and Mr. Tang into their home in Sacramento for dinner and fellowship. A couple of weeks later, they invited them to a large Vietnamese church in Southern California. After the church service, Mr. Tang was introduced to the pastor. The pastor asked if he wanted to accept Jesus into his heart. Mr. Tang nodded. Mai held her husband's hand, as he invited Love into his heart.

For several days, Mr. Tang didn't say a word. Then he called the elder and said he wanted to get rid of all his idols in his home and backyard. The pastor and the couple came, prayed, placed the idols in a box, and carried them out of the house.

Mai and her husband began to attend church regularly, and Mr. Tang found his spiritual gift—singing in the choir. On October twenty-third 2016, Pastor Tin of Christian Missionary Alliance Church baptized Mai and Mr. Tang into the family of God. I'm amazed how the love of God, from that old rugged cross, understood the wounded heart of a little Vietnamese girl, and brought her and her husband into eternity for His Glory. I'm so humbled to have played my part in His plan. His Love truly moves mountains. Trust in Jesus, give Him your silent obedience, and leave the rest to Love.

Lois Loofbourrow lives in Sacramento, California, and works full time. She's taking a break from writing to proudly support her adult son through mental health recovery and is an active member of NAMI.

THE BIGGEST STEP

Xochitl E. Dixon

Clutching the soft leather strap of my mocha tote, I stared at the silk, satin, and lace wedding dresses lining the farthest wall of the bridal shop. My right temple throbbed, as Mom gushed over gowns she insisted would be perfect for me. Reaching up to trace the swirls on another embroidered bodice, I winced.

Mom inspected another all-wrong-for-me dress. "You okay, Gabrielle?"

"Just sore from my workout." I coaxed a smile and rubbed my shoulder. "We've got lots to do before the big day."

She cupped my face with cool palms. "I'm so happy for you, honey. Jeremy can give you the life I've always dreamed of for you."

I opened my mouth to speak when Sarah, the extra-perky bridal consultant, stepped into our aisle. "Your dressing room is ready."

My Matron of Honor skirted around Sarah. "Sorry I'm late," said Brie. Smiling wide and sporting a spiky red pixie cut, she carried an oversized, overused, and definitely overstuffed black slouch purse. Brie squealed like a teenager glimpsing her favorite heartthrob at the mall. "Oh…my…gosh! Gabby, your hair looks fabulous!"

I touched my bare neck with mixed feelings. "I'm still getting used to it." I met my friend halfway down the long aisle flanked by a gaggle of gowns. "What's in that hunk of a handbag?"

"A surprise." She flung her arms around me. "You'll love it."

Brie's hug warmed me to the marrow of my aching bones. I inhaled her spritz-of-the-week, Japanese Cherry Blossom, and thanked God with a silent prayer. When I'd trudged into our Bible study group over a year ago, I never expected to meet the pint-sized burst of joy who would become the best friend I'd ever had.

Mom gave Brie a peck on the cheek. "I'm glad you made it, Briana. How's that handsome husband of yours?"

"God-fearing, kind, and hard-working. So, I'd say he's beyond amazing."

"And your beautiful boys?"

"Annoyingly taller than me. I'm trying to convince them to rise up and call me Blessed. But so far all they do is grunt and raid the refrigerator for snacks."

Mom laughed and plucked another so-not-what-I-would-pick dress off the rack. "Oh, Gabrielle, this one's lovely," she said, handing me a lace mermaid gown with cap sleeves.

Grinning, I widened my eyes when Brie met my gaze. We loathed cap sleeves, but I couldn't bear to hurt my mom's feelings.

Sarah swept in like a super-stealth ninja and took the dress from my arms. "Please follow me to dressing room four, Ladies."

Brie schooled us about the plight of Soccer Moms, as Sarah ushered us into a private lounge area with a platform and mirrors center stage. My mother settled into the cozy sofa as Brie pulled me into the changing room. "Get comfortable, Mrs. Gomez. The Matron of Honor gets to tuck and zip. But I've got a surprise for Gabby, too. So, we'll be a minute."

"I know you two." Mom pulled a novel out of her purse. "I came prepared."

We laughed as I closed the door behind us. I slumped into a plush leather loveseat. Closing my eyes, I pinched the bridge of my nose. *What am I doing, Lord?*

Brie swooshed hangers across the metal rod on the rack that held dream-dresses perfect for anyone but me. "You didn't pick any of these out," she said. "Did you at least pray about what we discussed last month?"

"Every day, as promised." *Lord, what am I supposed to do?* The silence squeezed my heart.

Kneeling in front of her purse, Brie pulled out a rectangular box. "Ignore the used birthday wrapping paper. It's all I had left." She stood, sat next to me, and handed me the present. "You'll need these, no matter what you decide."

I stared at the selection of dresses in front of us. "No easy choices here."

"Nope." She pointed to the homemade gift tag decorated with the words "God is my strength" scripted in calligraphy below my name. "It's the Hebrew meaning of Gabrielle."

"Brie–"

"I know. I'm the best. And no matter what you decide, I'll support you." She narrowed her eyes. "Unless you choose that hideous gown with the organza skirt."

Shaking my head, I unwrapped the box and stared at the red sequined sneakers. "You remembered."

"How could I forget?"

When I'd mentioned my favorite movie during Bible study, I'd said I wanted a pair of red shoes for days I felt lost.

Brie hugged my arm. "You'll find your way."

I slipped out of my sandals and into my sparkling shoes.

Her smile dimpled her cheeks. "If you're going to walk by faith, you need to…you know…walk. One step at a time. Even baby steps count."

I twisted the two-carat ring on my finger. "Our house will be ready for move-in…a week before we get back from Paris."

Brie nodded.

I'd invested six years with Jeremy. Six years. "Help me try on the strapless A-Line. It's the only one close to what I'd pick out."

Her smile didn't even come close to dimpling her cheek, as she prepared the dress.

I pulled my sweater over my head, grimaced, tossed it on the couch, and breathed through the pinch in my ribcage.

She dropped the dress when I turned toward her. "You lied," she said.

Adjusting the hem of my camisole, I picked up the crumpled gown. "It's the first time he ever—"

"Left a mark?"

"You don't—"

"Understand?" She swiped streaks of tears from her cheeks with the back of her hand. "I told you verbal abuse was a red flag."

"He promised—"

"It would never happen again? Did he blame you, too?"

I hugged the dress to my chest. The beads pressed into my forearms. "We've paid for the venue, the caterer, the cake, the flowers—"

"And?"

"RSVPs are pouring in."

She bowed her head. "It's not the first time, is it?"

I perched on the edge of the loveseat.

"Gabby, I told you what happened in high school. You can't really see my physical scars anymore. But you know God's still healing wounds caused by Kevin's verbal and emotional abuse, years after He helped me get out. It's even affected my marriage." Brie sat next to me. "You're not alone like I was."

I loosened my grip on the gown. When did I start accepting Jeremy's critical comments as truth? When did I start insisting I was fine, hiding the bruises, excusing his fits of rage, falling for his tears, believing his promises to change? Why didn't I leave after the first time he slapped me?

"Gabrielle."

I whispered, "God is my strength." *Help me, Lord.* I tugged the ring off my finger. "What am I going to tell my mother?"

"The truth." Brie placed her hand on mine. "The road's not easy or short. But the first step's the biggest, the hardest."

My sparkling red sneakers peeked out from beneath the hem of the satin skirt. I lifted my chin and smiled. "It's a good thing I've got a new pair of shoes."

*Xochitl (so-cheel) E. Dixon, an **Our Daily Bread** devotional writer, enjoys encouraging others, being married to her best friend, Alan, being a mom and a pet-parent, traveling, photography, and sharing God's truth and love. **The Biggest Step** won first place in the West Coast Christian Writers Contest in February 2017.*

THE LOVE-YOUR-NEIGHBOR WALK

Dana Sudboro

Surely, loving our neighbors includes sharing Christ—God's greatest gift of love.

Two by two, door to door? Hardly.

Although a former milk salesman showed me how to do that in the 1970s, with a spiritual-diagnostic questionnaire leading to a gospel presentation, the results were not impressive. At least not for me. Nor would I recommend the method today. Who but cult members pound the streets this way?

Far more recommended is friendship evangelism—that is, developing a relationship with neighbors and letting witnessing opportunities happen as they happen.

Soon after moving into our apartment complex, my wife invited our eight closest neighbors—three couples and two singles—over for supper. Three people came. That was, as Rick said in *Casablanca*, "the beginning of a beautiful friendship." Opportunities to share our faith have followed the way of love. Super naturally.

But how about the neighbors who live farther than borrowing-a-cup-of-sugar distance?

Our pastor shared a method that has proven amazingly rewarding—the prayer walk. He explained how for years the Lord led him in taking a walk for exercise and praying what the Spirit prompted for various households. So, I tried it.

In my old neighborhood, my habit had been to walk two miles a day for my health—doctor's orders. In this new neighborhood, I asked God to call attention to houses and guide me in what to pray for their occupants. This proved such a pleasure—trees, birds, sky, revelations, and all—that I've increased it to three and four miles.

Before you holler "mysticism," consider this. The Lord said, "My sheep hear my voice" (John 10:27 KJV). Hearing from heaven is as natural for believers as lambs bleating for their mother and leaping eagerly the moment they hear her voice— even when she's a mile away. Yes, I've seen it happen in Africa. Or, more in keeping with what Jesus said, it's as normal as a flock recognizing their shepherd's voice and coming when he calls.

Sometimes God speaks through metaphors. For example, a tall skinny evergreen rising from beside a house caught my eye. I prayed that, just as that tree pointed skyward, God would draw the occupants of that house to look up—see Him—whose glory fills the heavens. That they would begin to recognize Him, and thank Him for the blessings which shower down upon them every day.

Or, I pass someone walking their dog. After smiling and saying hi, I pray that God will reveal to them the Friend who sticks closer than a brother, who is more faithful and unconditional in His love than their favorite pet.

Often, it's a word that God brings to mind. "Reconciliation" led me to pray for the relationships in one household: parents with children, husband and wife. That forgiveness flow and heal every hurting heart.

It can also be a mental image. No, I don't walk with my eyes closed. But God can turn the sight of venetian blinds into a picture of a man sitting in an overstuffed chair in his den, book in hand, reflecting upon his life. "Lord," I pray, "draw him into Your word and reveal the wonderful plans You have for him."

Once, God drew my attention to a crème brulé house—a lovely combination of pale yellow siding and burnt amber roofing. "Give me a prayer," I asked.

"Rock hard," He said.

Whoa! The rule for a prayer walk, as for all ways of loving our neighbor, is to minister grace, not judgment or condemnation. Stumped, I started to pray, "God soften their hearts…" But no, that wasn't it.

God reminded me of what I'd seen on a visit to Placerville: a large black rock, sawn through, revealing a riot of royal purple crystals sparkling like jewels—yes, a geode, so massive and beautiful that the merchants were asking more than $1,000 for it.

"Lord," I prayed, "open their hearts to the splendor of Your love, and let its brilliance so transform their hearts that it shines forth for everyone around them to see."

What was the difference, you ask, between these two prayers? Apparently, what God had in mind was not a slow softening, like gentle showers falling on clumps of earth, but rather sudden revelation, like a bolt of lightning splitting a rock in two.

No, we can't always be sure what God is saying. But that's the joy and faith in it. What we can be certain of, is that God will do "exceedingly abundantly above all that we ask or think" (Ephesians 3:20 NKJV). Further, the Spirit "helps us in our weakness, for we do not know how we should pray, but the Spirit himself intercedes for us...according to God's will" (Romans 8:26-27 NET).

I find myself repeating certain prayers—God's promise to Joshua, for example—that the kingdom of God come to every neighborhood where I place my feet. Or, that the coming spiritual awakening, so often prophesied for the Sacramento area, will include "this family too" or "that apartment-full also."

Often, by the time I'm one or two miles into the walk, I'm floating on air—the peace of God spiriting me along like a feather on a breeze.

Perplexing at first, the words "be still" frequently came to mind. So, I prayed that God would still the hearts of the people living in the house I was passing. That He would free them from distractions, so they would hear His voice.

However, as these "be still" occurrences multiplied, I realized it wasn't for my neighbors, it was for me. Even if it took half a block of walking and waiting before I heard from heaven, that's what God wanted me to do. Sure enough, the revelation came, an inner knowing what to pray for the household I'd passed.

In other words, it's a learning experience—God teaching how to "pray prophetically," as some call it. Try it. You'll like it. As you walk in His love for your neighbors, He'll share secrets of His heart, not only for them, but also for your family at home, and you personally. Loving your neighbor is truly loving yourself.

Dana Sudboro served nineteen years (1987-2006) as an Assemblies of God missionary to Burkina Faso, West Africa. Now in retirement (2006-present) Dana teaches part-time at Epic Bible College in Sacramento and writes Christian romance novels. His latest novella, **Exit Cyrus***, is available both in paperback and ebook at* http://www.inspirewriters.com/books/exit-cyrus/

Amazing Grace, Amazing Love
Ramona Kelly

Have you ever been in love? I mean really in love—the head over heels, giddy, and can't stop thinking about them kind of love? Perhaps you sit up all night talking, just getting to know that person. Even their quirks seem charming and cute, and you can't seem to wipe that silly grin off your face. For most of us, this holds true.

Not so much for me, at least not for the first thirty years of my life.

Certain events in my past stunted this from coming forth. On the contrary, I was a very bitter, angry, and distrusting young lady. This led me to make more than a few very foolish choices. I built walls in my heart to defend against the pain life sometimes brings. This type of pain seems to target those of us who are vulnerable. Many times, these walls bring a contradictory outcome of what we hoped love was, and one that attracts injury rather than fulfillment. Oh yes, I was a mess.

Yet, when I least expected it, God entered my darkened heart and shined His light in the crevices of my pain. His gift of love and forgiveness brought forth healing. This love soothed and penetrated my damaged soul. Oh, the amazing love and grace of God!

I remember so clearly the night His cleansing swept over me. It was like wave upon wave of warm love oozing though my soul, the very core of my being, like the juice from a ripened plum on a warm summer day. I had not cried in years. Then the dam burst, tears flooded my eyes and flowed freely with such sorrow, wrenching my heart. Gradually this struggle turned into tears of joy! Oh, what amazing love abides in the Savior of our souls!

His forgiveness flooded my being. Then He told me I also had to forgive those who had damaged me. This was the beginning of total freedom, healing, and wholeness. There is so much power in forgiveness. As I gave Him each hurt—memories of those who had pierced my inner core—the walls in my heart began to melt like wax dripping down a candlestick.

As time passed, I continued to fall deeper in love with Jesus. I would seek opportunities to share His love and grace with others.

Years later, in Hawaii, I joined in a prison ministry with some friends, called "Victory Ohana," which translates to the "Victory Family." I became the director of the women's home. Actually, the women came to live in *my* home. Women who were fresh out of prison under a supervised released status, women coming off the streets, women coming out of the most detrimental abuse you can imagine. We all lived under one roof. They desperately needed a Savior and healing, just as God had healed me. I was so willing to be a vessel for the Master's use.

During this time, my youngest son was in elementary school. On one hand, he witnessed the power of God and being a part of helping others. On the other hand, the atmosphere began to shift. Rebellion and defiance was beginning to fill the air. The women would back-bite, grumble, and complain. They would argue with me about their concerns, from picking their clothes off the floor, to cleaning up after themselves, curfew, what not to watch on my TV, and the like. They wanted to know who made me the boss that they now had to abide by my rules. It's funny how easily one can forget where we came from, of the bondages we were in, and why we need help.

I would wake early in the morning and lay hands on each door, praying over the individuals on the other side. Some women would stay. Others would leave. I began to feel the weight of balancing *the home* and a semi-normal home life for my son. The stress began to weaken me.

Under all the pressure, some of the reactions of my past, the old ways, squeezed out of me and began to seep through. Yes, I had fallen in love with my Redeemer, but truthfully, I still loathed myself for the many horrid actions of my past. I was not only angry with the turmoil, but I was angry at me—how I was reacting to it. "Oh God," I cried over and over again, "What is happening to me?" How could this be? I didn't want to be like that. I hated it. I hated me. Yet there I was, acting a fool all over again.

Perplexed and feeling worthless again, God finally showed up. I was on the Potter's wheel. This was just another layer of the onion skin that He was peeling away from my tattered soul. He began to reveal to me that in spite of the fact He truly had forgiven me, and that I too, had forgiven others, I had not forgiven myself.

Instead, I hid the unforgiveness and tucked it away. Now, He was exposing it, so that I could truly be free.

Jesus said to him, "'You shall love the LORD your God with all your heart, with all your soul, and with all your mind.' This is the first and great commandment. And the second is like it: 'You shall love your neighbor as yourself.'" (Matthew 22:37-39 NKJV)

How could I love my neighbor, or anyone for that matter, if I had no love for myself? On the contrary, contempt and disdain was exposed in my behavior. As He enabled me, I was able to finally give this up to Him and forgive myself. Oh what love! What amazing love of the Father, that He continues to show to me.

I am so thankful for the lessons He teaches us through the storms of life. I have learned that in myself, I can do nothing, but with Him, all things are possible. The more time I spend with God and in His Presence, the more His Presence will get into me.

He who does not love, does not know God, for God is love. (1 John4:8 NKJV)

Yes, *Love is God.*

Do I feel giddy? At times I do, in the most enthusiastic of ways. He not only has turned my scoffing into a silly smile, but put peace in my soul and joy in my heart. I am head over heels in love with Jesus.

At times, I can spend hours just talking with Him, reading, studying, loving Him, worshiping, and basking in His Presence. I can't seem to get enough of Him.

Others times, like Peter, I falter and I fail, and then realize I have so many short comings. I think of one of favorite scriptures:

My grace is sufficient for you, for My strength is made perfect in weakness… (2 Corinthians 12:9 NKJV)

God is perfect. Unlike other loves we may encounter with quirks, God has none. He is perfect.

In my times of weakness, I can trust His promises. He will cause His strength to be perfected in me. He is faithful. He is trustworthy and He will never leave nor forsake me. In this I have found my perfect, true, and lasting love. I am loved.

Ramona Kelly recently joined Inspire Christian Writers group. She is so thankful and looks forward to learning and growing. She loves the Lord with all her heart. Ramona Kelly's passion is prayer and helping others, to give hope and encouragement, especially to women who have come out of an abusive past.

My First Love
Jasmine Schmidt

Forever my first love,
The man who held my heart,
Who cradled me in his arms,
And calmed me in the dark,
Whose voice sang me songs,
Deep into the starry night,
Whose fingers I clasped,
As I first began to walk…

Forever my first love,
The man who kept my heart,
Who waltzed away my fears,
When my soul grew heavy,
Who remained my constant,
Throughout the chaos of life,
And whose words of wisdom,
Sustained me night and day…

Forever my first love,

The man who gifted my heart,

As I became one with another,

With rings and sacred vows,

But always remember this,

Your place cannot be taken,

Because, Daddy, you are

Forever my first love.

Jasmine Schmidt is a children's and YA fiction writer as well as a poet. Writing is her passion and her calling. God gave her a talent with words, and she writes to bring Him glory. Jasmine's goal is to provide readers with clean, intriguing books and emotionally moving poems to enjoy.

Phantom Love

Michelle Janene

Jess slid onto a stool and slouched.

The blonde behind the counter nodded as smoothies whirled.

Jess hated the gym.

Soft brown eyes smiled from the end of the bar, as a man lifted his smoothie in her direction.

Was he smiling at her?

"Oh, he's cute," Rach said.

Jess turned with a sigh. Of course, he wasn't looking at her. Rachel Summers, her best friend, was exotic—straight raven hair, dark-chocolate eyes, and warm sun-kissed skin. Rach drew every eye.

"He's smiling this way."

"Of course, he is. You arrived." Jess failed to hide the jealousy in her voice.

Jess took the two smoothies from the waitress and handed one to Rach. They sipped in silence.

"Hello." His deep voice vibrated over Jess's skin.

Rach giggled. Their blossoming conversation never included Jess.

She finished her drink and disappeared into the locker room. A woman bumped her without an apology or a glance. She grew more invisible.

In front of her locker, she stared at her distorted reflection in the polished paint. That was truly her. A washed-out phantom no one noticed. All her friends, except Rach, were married. A few had babies. Jess had never even been on a real date.

She jerked open the door to stop the specter from staring, snatched her bag, and groaned, remembering the hunk she'd left talking to her friend. Rach would soon have a ring on her finger and Jess would be alone…again.

Heartbreak crushed her. Air stagnated in stone lungs. Tears stung but she refused to release them, as she clenched her lids tight. Her heart thundered, rattling her ribs, until the wave dissipated and she drew in a few steady breaths. These spells were coming more often.

Definitely time to leave.

She'd spend another depressing evening sitting on the couch with a romance novel, devouring her allotted low-fat chips. She'd never find a love like the stories in her novels. And truly, did it matter if she ate a half-gallon of chocolate ice cream? These months at the gym and refusing her favorite treats hadn't gotten her a single glance from anyone. She'd lost a whole dress size and bought new clothes. Still, she felt invisible.

Bag over her shoulder, she kicked the locker closed and stomped out.

Bible verses bombarded her, as rays of the setting sun blocked out the rows of cars.

For I know the plans I have for you. Plans to prosper you and not to harm you, plans to give you a hope and a future.

"Where is my hope? My future?"

It is not good for the man to be alone.

But it's all right for me? The pain pierced again, stealing her breath. She reached for the wall to keep from falling.

"Freeze!"

Jess's head shot up and she scanned the parking lot. Lights flashed to her left at the end of the lot near the bank. Cops stood behind car doors, guns drawn. A suspect faced them with a woman in his grasp, a gun to her head. People ran toward Jess in an attempt to escape the line of fire.

She stared, paralyzed.

The gunman shouted back at the officers…words she couldn't understand.

I should do something. The thought snapped across her mind like a breaking rubber band.

She blinked twice, dropped her bag, and rummaged through it for anything of use. But, it wasn't like she carried dumbbells around. An idea took root. She pulled out her windbreaker.

Leaving her bag on the pavement, she crept behind a row of cars.

The bank robber yelled obscenities and inched back toward the door to re-enter the bank, but the guard had locked it to protect those still inside.

"Release the hostage. There's nowhere to go."

Jess tiptoed nearer before the cops closed around him. This was insane, but what did she have to lose?

The sobbing captive probably had a family or at least a boyfriend. *Who would miss me?* Other than Rach, there wasn't a soul who would even mark Jess's absence.

Jess rose silently behind the gunman. Some of the cops gazed in amazement at her daring approach. She moved forward. Using her jacket like a lasso, she flipped it over his gun hand and jerked back. At the same moment, she wrapped her other arm around his throat and jumped on his back. "Run!"

A shot rang out.

The robber shook free, and whirled.

Another shot! Maybe there were several.

She was thrown back against the wall next to the ATM. Had he punched her in the gut?

He stared, unblinking.

She stared back, the taste of bitter metal washing over her tongue.

As if in slow motion, his body slumped to the ground.

In this same suspended time, she lifted her hand and gazed at her red soaked fingers. Her vision blurred and swirled as orders exploded around her.

"Get an ambulance!"

"Secure the shooter!"

"Check for other assailants!"

Her legs buckled. Surrounded in a haze of flashing colors, she slid down the wall, landing hard.

"Hold on. Help's coming." His face was etched with concern. His hand trembled as he placed it on top of hers to stem the escaping gush. She tipped to the side and he caught her with his other hand, easing her down to the pavement beside him. His blue eyes were intense. "Stay with me, beautiful. Stay with me."

He turned away to shout for the ambulance again. But he had seen her—looked at her—noticed her! *He called me beautiful.*

She couldn't fight the tears.

He caressed her cheek, brushing away the tears. "It'll be alright, just hang in there." He continued to cradle her cheek. "I'm Mark. What's your name?"

She let the breath ease from her. Someone had at last seen her.

"Jess!" Rach screamed, but it was far away.

She let go.

❦

A steady beeping dragged Jess back from oblivion. It annoyed her and she tried to squirm away.

A hand tightened over hers, large and strong. A rough thumb rubbed over the back of her hand as it held hers firm. "You coming back, beautiful?"

The voice caressed her as much as the hand.

She pried her eyes open only to be stabbed by shafts of light.

"Here, let me fix that." The hand pulled from hers.

A cold shudder raced up her arm. Footsteps moved away and the light leaking in around her lids dimmed. She dared open them again.

A broad-shouldered man stood silhouetted against the light of the blinds he'd just closed. He returned to her hospital bed and brushed her cheek. "Welcome back." His blue eyes washed over her.

She knew him, didn't she?

"Oh my gosh, you're awake." Rach rushed over and snatched up the hand he'd been holding.

"I'll give you ladies a moment. Anyone thirsty?" He pointed to Rach, "Coffee, two creams?"

She nodded as Jess wrinkled her nose.

"No coffee for you. Lemonade? Don't know if you're allowed, but I'll ask." He disappeared before she could answer.

"Who…?" The words choked in her parched mouth.

Rach turned and looked toward the door. "Mark?"

Mark. She knew that name too.

"He's the cop that stayed with you." Rach's hands perched on her hips. "After you went all *Die Hard* on the bank robber and rescued the hostage."

Memories flooded back in a rush.

"He hasn't left your side. He waited with me while you were in surgery. Been parked here ever since."

"Why?"

Rach shrugged. "Love."

"I don't even know him." Jess coughed. "Or him, me." Was her mouth getting drier?

"Get out of your head, Jess. You're not me. I love to flirt, like bees to honey in the beginning, but then I lose interest. Don't know that I'll ever settle down. You, it will be one and done, girlfriend." She winked. "And, I like this one."

Mark returned with three cups between his hands. He set them on the table at the end of her bed. "Sissy coffee," he said handing one to Rach. "Watered juice for the pretty one." He came toward her.

She tried to sit up. Pain exploded across her middle.

"Don't. Belly wounds are brutal. Relax." His hand slid under her head, cradling it gently as he raised her and brought the cup to her lips.

He sat and they talked, but he only had eyes for Jess. For once it was as if Rach wasn't in the room.

⁂

"Hello, Doctor. Has there been any change?" Rachel entered the hospital room where her best friend had been lying asleep for two weeks.

"Sorry, Miss Summers. Her condition hasn't changed. Though not exactly in a coma, she won't wake. Her eyes move like she's dreaming. She even smiles at times."

"Jess has always lived too much in her head." Rachel took the seat beside the bed and squeezed her friend's hand.

Jess smiled.

"At least they're happy dreams." Rach held tight. "Come on Jess, wake up. The real world needs you."

Michelle writes Christian fantasy and lives with two dogs and numerous fictional characters. She leads two critique groups and owns Strong Tower Press to publish her own works and assist other Indie authors. Her passion is to sprinkle God's truths in every possible realm. Visit her at www.strongtowerpress.com

SHARING MY HERO ON MOTHER'S DAY

Denise Lee Branco

My mother's love for animals runs deep within her soul. She seems connected to God's creatures through a language only she and God share. And though every day is Mother's Day in my mind, as the Lord continues to grace my life with her presence, this year I proudly honor my mom's blessing on the life of an especially grateful feline.

My mom comes from the day and age when you knew all of your neighbors by name and you all looked out for one another. Today, her spirit is unchanged. Even the neighborhood pets are on a first-name basis with her.

One stormy mid-April day, a disheveled and gaunt feline wandered along a busy road. This never-before-seen weather-beaten cat stole Mom's heart. She asked her neighbors if they recognized the cat and knew its owner. No one could provide any information about the cat. So, mom began to feed it on her front porch because she couldn't bear to let it go hungry. Mom hoped that by feeding it, she'd eventually earn the cat's trust, catch it, and find out if it was microchipped.

The homeless kitty couldn't resist the temptation of fresh food. At first, he would use the cover of darkness to drop by and lick the bowl clean. He then added breakfast to his daily meal plan. Soon, the meandering feline's days on the road ended.

On the morning of April 28, 2017, the cat arrived for his usual hearty breakfast. This time, instead of the typical eat and run scenario, he basked in the warmth of the morning sun upon the ground which allowed Mom to get close. The two struck up a conversation. Cat had much to say. Perhaps words of thanks to my mom. Or, perhaps he sensed God in the process of helping him, through my mom, to find his way back home.

Mom had already contacted her retirement community lost pets coordinator and had arranged to borrow the microchip scanner which is available to residents at no charge. With that in mind, Mom coaxed the cat into the garage with wet food. Once there, my mom wanted to give a lady named Becky, who showed interest in the cat after seeing my lost pet photo on social media, the first chance to see him because her adored fur baby, Milo, had been missing for months. Both Mom and Becky hoped with all their being that this homeless kitty was him.

The ladies coordinated a visit to my mom's home later that same day to see if this kitty might be Becky's Milo. Now, with the cat in Mom's garage, the hopeful reunion was expedited. Becky arrived and discovered that the cat was not Milo. Mom's tears flowed. She was heartbroken. She longed for a happy reunion...one of many months in the making.

Seeing Mom so distraught, Becky kindly offered to take the cat to Field Haven Feline Rescue for microchip scanning, where they were able to identify him as Tyler. They also discovered he'd been missing from his owner, David, for five months. Field

Haven Feline Rescue volunteers coordinated Tyler's reunion with his papa later that day. From what Becky told me, Tyler had lots to say to his papa about their five-month separation. Wouldn't you?

Their reunion was no accident. I love to remember how everything led to that moment. My mother had asked me to drop by her home after work the previous Wednesday because she was out of town and needed me to refill the rabbit food container and the backyard bird feeder. Yes, she feeds wild birds and cottontail bunnies, which for me is a heartwarming reminder of how much my mother loves animals. If she hadn't asked me to go to her home that day, I wouldn't have run into Tyler during his dinnertime and had the opportunity to take photos of him to post on social media. My mother doesn't own a cellular smartphone or use a computer. However, because I do, I am thrilled that I had the opportunity to play a role in Tyler's journey home. We wouldn't have met Becky, who not only assisted mom in getting Tyler microchip scanned, but is a Field Haven Feline Rescue volunteer.

When my mother learned that Tyler was back home with his family, she became ecstatic, even though she misses seeing him on her porch and giving him tender loving care. That's because she knows how it feels to have a beloved lost pet safely returned.

When Mom was a child, she had a hefty, white-bibbed, orange long-haired cat named Mickey who was a loyal childhood companion. They shared a language based on mutual dependability and love. Every afternoon, Mickey made the long trek down their country drive to welcome Mom home from school. She could always count on Mickey to be there to greet her after a long day of studying. They'd chat, and then she'd pick him up to embrace him and carry him all the way back home.

One dreadful day, Mom returned from school to a barren driveway. Mickey was nowhere to be seen. My mother's heart dropped. Anguish and panic overwhelmed her as she searched for him around her home. Where was Mickey?

My mom's heartache continued for weeks. Then one day, she received a tip from the daughter-in-law of her dad's former male boss. Turns out, Mickey was being held prisoner in the cellar of that man's house. The news shocked my mom, and yet, she felt relieved that Mickey had been located. Their reunion was deeply touching in every sense of the word.

Just as the angels ensured Mickey made it safely back home to my mother those many years ago, I feel Mom became Tyler's first guardian angel. After five months on the road, God led Tyler to the person He knew loved animals and would care for him. Tyler probably met other angels before he returned home, but I feel Tyler's journey was divinely orchestrated because of my mom's spirit and love of animals.

I have witnessed this pure love. My mom's never-ending compassion and caring spirit for God's creatures makes me incredibly proud of her. She has always been and will continue to be my hero, not only on Mother's Day, but every day. This year, however, I'm pretty sure Tyler also considers my mom his hero.

*Denise Lee Branco is the award-winning author of **Horse at the Corner Post: Our Divine Journey,** and an inspirational speaker who continues to believe, dream, and overcome so those who meet her recognize the possibilities within them. Her memberships include literary and publishing organizations. Follow Denise on Twitter @DeniseLeeBranco and visit www.* DeniseInspiresYou.com

SMELLS LIKE RAIN

Loretta Sinclair

The sun hung high in the sky and shone brightly on the baseball diamond full of children. Meagan sat in the bleachers and watched her daughter play t-ball with the other kids. Smaller and weaker than the others her own age, Samantha battled to keep up, laughing and having more fun than the rest.

"She's a real gem," Wendy leaned in to whisper. "She was a preemie, right?"

Meagan smiled and nodded. Pride welled up inside of her at the sight of her little fighter on the field.

"How old was she when she was born?"

"Eighteen weeks. Less than one pound." She smiled. "Sixty-two weeks in the hospital."

Wendy put her arm around her friend and managed an awkward sideways hug. "Amazing she survived."

Meagan wiped away a tear. "The doctors didn't think she would. Our pastor was called in several times."

"I can't even imagine the pain and heartache of seeing your own child in an incubator like that."

Meagan nodded. "When she was born the nerve endings in her skin weren't fully developed yet, so we couldn't even hold her. It was excruciating. I've never heard screams like that before. I wanted so badly just to touch her, but the doctors wouldn't allow it."

"It's a miracle." Wendy took Meagan's hand in hers. "Thank you, God."

"Mommie, look! I'm batting!"

"I'm watching sweetie!" The two women refocused on the field. The ball was placed on the rubber tee, and Sam stepped up to the plate. The bat wavered awkwardly over her right shoulder for a moment, and she swung. It technically qualified as a hit because the bat touched the ball, although it was more of a bump and a fall. That didn't matter to the small girl with big dreams. She took off running as fast as her little legs would carry her toward first base while the other team scrambled for the loose ball.

"Safe!" the first base coach yelled. The crowd of moms roared.

"Good job, baby girl! I'm proud of you!" Meagan stood and waved to make sure her little runner could see her. After they made eye contact, she sat and talked with the other moms. As each kid stepped up to bat, the respective mom would cheer, and the others applauded. One for all, and all for one.

As the afternoon drew on, and the game came to a close, storm clouds drifted in. The coach huddled the kids all together and gave his post-game pep talk. He struggled to keep the attention of the giddy girls and rambunctious boys. After only a few moments they began to scatter, while the coach was still talking.

Samantha ran to the bleachers and launched herself into her mother's open arms. "Did you see me, Mommie? I ran all the way around the bases!"

"I saw, Sammie. I'm so proud of you!"

"Yeah." The child smiled big, missing teeth on the top, and a pink tongue showing through the hole. "Oh! Coach is talking. I need to go back."

The moms all laughed. Sam jumped off the bleachers, then stopped. She turned back. "Do you smell Him?"

"What, honey?"

Sam pointed at the rain clouds off in the distance. "There?"

"Oh, the rain? Yes, I can smell it."

"Yeah!" Sammie bubbled over. "It smells just like Him when He holded me in the hospital."

A lover of God and lover of words, Lori Sinclair is a single parent, working mom, and both a business and fiction author. Her dream is to retire one day and be a full-time author.

Marriage Delayed

Sandra Trezise-Heaton

It still seems like a dream, my wedding. I admire the rings on my finger. The diamonds sparkle in the sunlight with every movement of my hand. I often become transfixed by the display, fascinated by the way the light reflects the facets. I move my hand more than is needed to accomplish a task or carry on a conversation. "Look everyone," I seem to say, "I belong. I am one of you. I am loved by a wonderful man. I am finally a grownup."

It may seem like I am a woman who got married just to have a flashy ring and be part of society. Let me assure you that is not the case. I waited a long time for the right person. I prayed. I cried. I dated and even got engaged several times. There was always a part of me that cautioned, *This is not right. He is not for you. You will not be happy.*

I have come to believe God protected me from myself many times. In my defense, everyone else was getting married. Why not me? My closet groaned under the weight of ghastly bridesmaid dresses. The purchase of wedding gifts and, eventually, baby gifts depleted my meager bank account. Each decade that passed—twenty, thirty, forty, heart-stopping fifty—I felt more alone, more lost, more a failure. I sang my favorite refrain, "It's my turn," at the top of my lungs. After all, didn't God know how old I was?

When I was in my twenties, a doctor told me that I probably would never have children. My heart sank with the loss of my dream for a family.

I looked for divorced men with children. Surely that was how God planned for me to be a mother. Often, bitterness over their broken marriages spilled over onto me. It became tiresome, being punished for another woman's perceived sins. God and I both knew I could commit enough of my own sins without carrying those of someone else.

God had not abandoned me, though at times it felt as if He had. He opened some very exciting doors for me during my single years. I taught overseas, traveled to nearly every continent, and had the chance to discover my spiritual gifts: teaching, music, writing, hospitality, counseling. In retrospect, the time was a valuable growth period.

I was definitely not pining away, except when a new decade birthday arrived. As those milestones came and went, I began to doubt my worth. "Why am I so alone? What is wrong with me?" It didn't help that I was increasingly on the outside of social events where a single woman was not on the guest list.

Work became my world. For a person who enjoys relationships and laughter, it was deadly. I became very serious, very sad, then depressed. My light went out.

I refused to date any more. My standards for dating had become so low that each man I dated was a little worse than the one before. Surrender was a struggle. What if the next man I met was the one? Didn't I need to be out there looking?

God sent me His answer through Jeremiah 29:11, *For I know the plans I have for you, declares the Lord, plans to prosper you and not to harm you, plans to give you hope and a future.*

My heart was changed by these ancient words from the prophet, Jeremiah. I desired to know what else life and God might have planned for me. Obviously, it was not marriage.

With my surrender, I became open to God's healing process. Like all surgery, it hurt. At times, it was excruciating. I needed to be stripped of the parts of my life that did not bear fruit and there were many.

God started with my desire to be in control of my life. My carefully set out plan was not His. It needed to be torn out of my hands that held tight to beliefs, wounds, and desires that kept me from God's best. He wanted everything—family, friends, pride in my reputation at work and in the community. The battle left me depleted, stunned and with no alternative but to surrender to God's grace.

It was in this place of weakness that He began to rebuild my life and heal the damage inflicted by poor decisions—my own and those who had harmed me. He gave me the ability to forgive myself as well as others.

Now that I am on the other side of the struggle, I realize that God was preparing me for the wonderful man I was to marry, and the challenges that marriage brings. I am a very different person than I was twelve years ago. I have the gift of perspective. Most of my life has already passed. The questions, strivings, and yearnings of youth have either disappeared or are resolved. I can look back and see much of what God has done and acknowledge the wisdom of His plan. What I don't see remains a mystery and I am finally at peace with that.

Sandra Trezise-Heaton is retired and traveling often with her husband. Her creative non-fiction has been published in three Inspire anthologies and several caregiver magazines.

LOVINGKINDNESS

Edward L. Wright

Lord, I'm unworthy of Your lovingkindness
and the faithfulness You have shown.

Your strength and wisdom constantly guide me,
for I never walk alone.

In the midst of my trials, You gently hold my hand.

Rescuing me from dangers
upon Your every sovereign command.

Lord, You've always been patient, merciful, and kind.

Despite all my inadequacies, Your abundant
love isn't hard to find.

Continue to shape and mold me into a fruitful vessel.

Give me wisdom, strength, and courage,
where I won't have to wrestle.

Give me the discernment to go out among the masses
to evangelize Your Word,

By sharing with everyone what I've seen and heard.

Give me the strength to walk obediently
on the precepts of what You've taught,

Guiding me ever steadily without a second thought.
Help me to leave a testimony of what You did for me,
So others will know how encouraged they can be.

Born in Tucson, Arizona, Dr. Edward L. Wright
spent most of his early years in Denver, Colorado.
He is the youngest of eight siblings. As a child,
he enjoyed reading various literary authors such
as James Baldwin, Richard Wright, Gwendolyn
Brooks, and Countee Cullen.

PERFECT LOVE BRINGS CHANGE

Tessa Bertoldi

Have you been hurt by someone you loved—a friend, coworker, spouse, parents? Have there been great hurts, trauma, and unforgiveable pain? Perhaps the unforgiveable is a million tiny cuts that bleed and never heal.

While I carried the scars of my pain, I could not move past them. I cultivated seeds of pain, dragging around the past like an overpacked suitcase without wheels. I needed those who were involved to acknowledge my pain and innocence. I played the dialogues over and over in my head, reinforcing the pain to keep it fresh.

I believed in God's grace and free gift of forgiveness for sin. I held fast to the knowledge that God loved me in my damaged state. My soul was safe and had been pardoned, but what had I done with that pardon? Christ had paid for my pardon with his life, his perfect life. Never did he bring up my part, my bad choices, or the continual hurt I did to myself and others. I could not see, I was blind and angry at the many injustices. The judgements came from Satan and misguided people who constantly bring up flaws, faults, and negatives. It was a good way of keeping the pain fresh and me distracted from loving God and his creation.

Therefore, there is now no condemnation for those who are in Christ Jesus, because through Christ Jesus the law of the Spirit who gives life has set you free from the law of sin and death. (Romans 8:1-3)

God continued to love and provide a way for me, even when I could not see it. He went before me and cleared obstacles, blessed me with a beautiful daughter and my beloved Mr. Man. Still, I was hurting and angry. I only allowed myself short periods of freedom from pain. God had pardoned me, but I still lived like a prisoner. As long as I was continually cataloguing the wrongs and hurts, I could not heal.

Then I said something cruel I cannot even remember. I do remember the look on Mr. Man's face, the pain I inflicted, the tears that fell silently down his face. He never said a word, never lashed back at me. He just waited with pain and love in his eyes. I begged his forgiveness, but my eyes had been opened. If he had yelled back at me, I would never had heard God speaking to me.

...but do not have love, I gain nothing. Love is patient, love is kind. It does not envy, it does not boast, it is not proud. It does not dishonor others, it is not self-seeking, it is not easily angered, it keeps no record of wrongs. Love does not delight in evil but rejoices with the truth. It always protects, always trusts, always hopes, always perseveres. (1 Corinthians 13:3-7 NIV)

I knew this scripture, had memorized it, but I had not lived it. The pain I had inflicted on my beloved did not demonstrate my love for him or my God. I was devastated, did I really believe I was pardoned? I did not believe I was worthy or deserving, and I was right. The pain crowded out love and my ability to really love deeply.

I withdrew and sought time to understand. God reminded me He did not retaliate, and just like my beloved had shown me the depth of His love by patiently loving me, God patiently waited for me to be ready to let go of the dialog and the pain. He wants His best for me. I had to let go of the catalog of pain, and trust in Him. I had been a victim for so long, I forgot to be a survivor. Christ had lovingly broken the chains and pardoned me. I had tried to put the broken pieces back together, time and time again. Christ brought no accusations and even provided me with a flesh and blood example of what real love looked like. It was a very short leap from my beloved's love and forgiveness to the love and forgiveness of my Heavenly Father.

It has not been easy to let go of injustice and forgive. It is easy to remember that the way of Christ is to forgive when forgiveness is not earned. I am not the only person who has experienced a hurt, why have I been so selfish to keep the free gift of forgiveness to myself? Why have I carefully kept forgiveness covered in pain to obscure it from the world?

I had plenty of help. Satan is a great deceiver and wants us to be victims, never survivors. He wants us trapped in our pain, incapable of showing love to others. Now you know as well as I did. Can you lay down your hurts and pick up His love? The first thing He wants to hear from us is our invitation to ask Him to be the Lord of our lives, to acknowledge we fail and accept His forgiveness.

I challenge you to find a place to be alone with God. Be still and think about how He has pardoned you and broken the bonds of sin. Then talk with Him. Yell at Him if you need to, He can take it. Go ahead and tell Him what you are mad about, all your hurts, all your complaints—you know, the ones you've saved up for years. Even the ones you hide from yourself! He will listen and is drama-and-gossip safe, the ugly spiral of accusations can be broken. He will love you as you learn to stop the accusations and show His love to others.

If you are less than perfect like me, you will begin the catalog again and will need to repeat the process of sacrificing hurt and pain. God will be waiting, He remains perfect, loving, and forgiving. He will take each hurt as you release them. He will return peace and love to you. I now wake up each day looking forward to what the day will bring. Gone are the days of dark oppressive doom and depression hanging over me like a thundercloud. I thank Him daily for His pardon and the knowledge that when my days are done, I will be with Him in paradise. Where are you today? Victim or survivor, drama or peace, prisoner or set free? Remember, life is not perfect, but His love is.

Tessa Bertoldi, a secret writer through school and years as a Risk Manager, a mom and Technical Writer. Set free, her current efforts include a post-apocalyptic sci-fi novel, work with the National Novel Writing Month and Staff Volunteer for the San Francisco Writer's Conference. Her next life chapters promise to be even more exciting.

Loves Me, Loves Me Not...

Ellen Cardwell

Little girls get crushes on little boys. To find out if our little man feels the same way, we play a guessing game. It's easy. All we have to do is pick apart a doomed daisy one petal at a time. Will the last petal be a "he loves me" or a "he loves me not?"

Little boys have their own methods of detection: accidentally bumping into us, grabbing something of ours and playing "keep away," or having a friend pass us a note that says he likes us. How we respond—with a smile or frown—lets him know how we feel.

Shall we leave it up to the daisy to determine if he's "the one?" Or shall we try a juvenile ploy to find out what she thinks of me? Of course not. We adults wouldn't think of it. We know better, or so we say. We'll just *know* when the *right* one comes along.

But, will we? Unfortunately, marriages don't always last, and that's true for Christians and non-Christians alike. The emotional, physical, and rational attractions that brought us together originally aren't always enough to keep our relationship vital in the long run.

So how is a person to know? The heartthrob we saw through rose-colored glasses has flaws we overlooked before, but now they bother us. We aren't perfect, either. Adverse circumstances can bring out the best, or worst, in us. Good intentions fade, promises aren't kept, we let each other down. What we hoped would be heaven on earth can become a miserable, no-win situation.

Then why bother? Why take the risk of entering a life-long commitment at all? Let's just live together, play house, and see if we're compatible. Why not? Because, if we do, we're purposely settling for less than the ideal.

There's another consideration—one that takes a longer view. It includes the spiritual quotient of the individual we have feelings for. Are they committed disciples? Are the Scriptures their authority for living? Is their primary motivation to serve God, to discover and do His will for their lives? If the answer is yes to all three, that person has the right foundation on which to build a marriage.

I realize that not everyone wants to get married, or will. But if you do hope to share your life with someone, do you think God will handpick a spouse for you? Or is that a romantic notion we wish were true, but don't think is realistic?

We know there was one couple God created for each other—Adam and Eve. Even so, it wasn't long before they messed up their ideal situation and brought trouble on themselves. The perfect couple wasn't perfect for long!

That fact should let us off the perfection-hook. Even if we find the "perfect" person, we may not get together because they're looking for the perfect person, too. And we're not!

I think God brought my husband and I together, but we had to work through our differences just the same. We came from dissimilar backgrounds and had unrealistic expectations of each other. But loving God was the glue that kept us together.

My daughter and I were talking about my husband, to whom she always compared the men in her life, to their detriment. Hoping to take the edge off her idealism, I took a chance at painting a more realistic picture of him for her.

"He wasn't always like the way he is now. Actually, he was kind of a geek when we first met."

"What?" Her voice shot up an octave as her eyebrows rose. "How did you know he'd turn out the way he did?"

"I didn't."

"Then you really took a gamble when you married him," her voice quavered at the realization.

"I guess you could look at it that way. But I saw it as a step of faith."

"Hmmm," she responded, drawing into herself to ponder that idea.

I continued, "Both of us wanted to get married, and we wanted it to last, so we put the choice of our mate in the Lord's hands. Your dad was interested in someone else when we first met, and I was dating other guys. We would compare notes on our "progress," becoming good friends in the process. One day he noticed my eyes were sparkling, and it hit us both at the same time—we could stop looking any further. We'd found each other!"

"I hope that happens to me," she sighed, ending the conversation at that point. I could have continued, but she had shut down and moved on.

I could have told her about the aptitude tests we took and that the scores showed we had strengths where the other didn't and vice-versa, that the graphs of the results put side by side resembled gears that worked in concert. But that's not something that everyone can expect.

Yes, I believe God delights in bringing His children together when they let Him do the leading and choosing. That way, we're not dependent on human love alone to make our marriage work, because the love of Christ steps in when ours runs out. No matter what happens to us, we know we can make it with His help, and we never have to wonder if he or she loves me or loves me not. In Christ, the answer is always He loves me!

*Ellen Cardwell has been published in **The Upper Room Magazine**, **Heavenly Company: Entertaining Angels Unaware**, **Journeys to Mother Love**, several Inspire anthologies, **El Dorado Hills Telegraph**, and **Around Here Magazine**. Her first book, **American Proverbs**, was published in 2017 and is available on Amazon.*

The Ultimate "Love Like No Other"
Meredith Houston Carr

When I first found out I was going to be a mom, the joy nearly overwhelmed my happy heart. After several years of waiting, it was finally my turn to experience the "love like no other" my friends and Hallmark had told me about for so long.

My clueless mind imagined that once this baby arrived, I would float on "Cloud 9" for the rest of my life, buoyed by the smell of sweet baby skin, adorable clothes, and innumerable kisses. And when my firstborn arrived, all cries and perfect baby preciousness, I did indeed experience an unspeakable love. The smell of his sweet baby skin robbed me of breath, and I marveled at how it took mere seconds to fall madly in love with this brand new human being.

The love of a mother for her child is indeed a beautiful, mysterious thing…and yet, as time would teach me, there exists another side to this "love like no other"—a side that doesn't exactly have a place among the shiny, tingly Hallmark cards—because, along with the glorious ups of motherhood, come the painful lows of motherhood, the *hard love* of mothering.

At the tender age of three, and after many months of testing and wondering (with a heaping side of denial), this beloved firstborn of mine received a diagnosis of Autism Spectrum Disorder, or ASD. Those three little letters shook me to the core and sent me hurtling down the path of hard love. I found myself grieving what I *thought* motherhood would be and the child I *thought* my son would be. Instead, I began the journey of falling in love with the child God created him to be.

In the sad, blurry days following my son's diagnosis, I would toss and turn late into the night, a million and one questions pinging across my tired brain.

God, why would You choose me to mother a child with ASD? I'm not cut out for it! How will I know what to even do for him? I'm not like these bulldog-persistent-warrior moms I see out there! I'm quiet and reserved and don't even know where to begin. I don't want to fail him!

It's easy for us moms to fall down the rabbit hole of doubting ourselves and wondering if we're doing everything we should and could be doing for our children…and I've found this to be especially true in moms of kids with special needs.

Yes, these circumstances overwhelmed my heart with doubt and fear…but a funny thing happened in those sad and blurry days. A deep and primal love for my son began overwhelming my heart, *more* than the fear and doubt. I experienced a true love like no other, the kind that kicks in amidst the lowest of lows and compels you to go to the ends of the earth for your child. I found myself reading, researching, calling various resources, and reaching out to people—me, a classic introvert!

While we are just at the beginning of our son's journey, I'm beginning to see that all these amazing moms of special needs kids aren't simply *born*—they're *made*, through the beautiful and painful process of walking a different road of motherhood. It's the road of fashioning beauty from ashes. It's the road of attending therapies and appointments more than play dates and parties. It's being compelled by a love so strong, you couldn't stop it even if you tried.

This hard love means continuing on another day, even when you're so tired it feels like you might collapse. It means putting one foot in front of the other, even though you'd rather lock yourself in the bathroom and cry. It's giving more of yourself, even after it seems as though there's nothing left to give.

And while many days I wish for all the world this wasn't our path, I want my son to *know* the love I have for him. I want him to know that, no matter how hard the road ahead, no matter what challenges and heartaches he will face, we will face them together. I will always walk by his side. As long as I have breath in my body, he can count on my steadfast love for him.

Because the truth is, love of any kind isn't always easy—and it oftentimes looks quite different than we thought it would. Children push you to the brink. Wedding day joy fades with the years of struggles and trials. Friendships change with the passing of seasons. Others are not always easy to love, just as *we* are not always easy to love.

Everyone wants an enduring, "love like no other." Incredibly, our Heavenly Father answers our desire with His steadfast love for us. Though we test and try and push and doubt Him at times, His unwavering love for us never falters. Though we give Him reason to lock Himself away from us, He never will and never *could*—even in the lowest of lows.

On the cross, He gave us all of Himself in the greatest act of love this world has ever seen. Indeed, though our love as mothers and fathers for our children is fierce, it is but a shadow of the love the Father has for us. Isaiah 49:15 says:

Can a mother forget the baby at her breast and have no compassion on the child she has borne? Though she may forget, I will not forget you!

What a promise! And it's a promise we can count on, one in which we can place our hope. Just as I long for my son to be certain of my love for him, so our Heavenly Father longs for us to *know that we know that we know* that He loves us.

Are you living in the reality of God's unconditional, steadfast love for you today? What would it look like for you to absorb this truth and sink into the ultimate love like no other?

Rest assured, we will have difficult seasons, those unsuitable for a warm and fuzzy Hallmark card—but we will *always* have the assurance that God is working all things together for those who love Him, who have been called according to His purpose (see Romans 8:28). And truth be told, that is all the warm and fuzzy we will ever need.

Meredith Carr is a wife to one sweet husband and mom to three energetic children. An attorney in her former life, she now enjoys the thrilling, slightly crazy, stay-at-home-mom life. You can find her writing during naptime and in between loads of laundry.
Connect at www.meredithhcarr.com.

The Journey

Mary A. Allen

The journey so far had challenged her, with much of it up hill. There was, of course, the beautiful scenery along the way to consider, and the much-needed companionship was appreciated. But, none of it prepared her for the turn in the path. There weren't any mountains on the horizon. The road was flat, the sun bright and she was in good company.

She felt his love surrounding her when she closed her eyes and inhaled the fragrant flowers. When she opened them, a tunnel loomed in front of her, dark, and foreboding. No light emanated from the other end. Was this a cave? She stopped short.

"What's this?" she said to her loved one.

"Part of the journey."

Her eye twitched. "I don't want to go in there."

"It's part of the journey."

"*You* go," she said with a dismissive wave.

"I've already been there. I know the way."

"It's too dark. I don't want to go in there. I can't see the end." Her mouth pulled to the side and she bit her lip.

"I'll go with you. You have nothing to fear."

A slight nudge on her back encouraged her to move forward. She resisted, but the pressure continued.

"Please, I don't want to go. Can't we climb over the mountain instead?" Her voice whined through the still air.

"I'm right here beside you. Let's go."

Though her feet never moved, she was surrounded by blackness. She could no longer see the one she loved. Her lips trembled.

"I'm frightened. I can't see you." Her heart thudded and she could hardly breathe.

"I'm here. Listen to my words. I will guide you through the darkness."

"What if there's a huge pit and I fall in?" A knot tightened deep within her chest.

"Listen to me. I'm here. Continue straight ahead."

She started to cry. Hot tears streamed down her face. She bent over, resting her hands on her thighs and sobbed. "Why do I have to be here?"

"Remember what I said. I will not leave you. I love you. We will make this journey together."

The pressure on her back returned. She stood and took several more steps through the inky expanse. Her breaths came in heaving waves. Nausea threatened with every unknown step. She looked back. No light from the entrance. No soothing fragrance. Just the cold, dank blackness.

She tripped and fell, and sat in the muddy dirt sobbing. "I want to go back. I don't want to be on this journey anymore."

The silence rang in her ear like a siren. It was so oppressive she tried to scream above it. "I don't want to be here," she shrieked. There was no response. "Hey, are you there? You told me you wouldn't leave me."

She picked herself up and took a step. "Are you there?" She waved her arms in frantic circles in search of him. Warm blood ran down her shins. She leaned over to touch her knees. The wounds burned. What if she got an infection? There was no way to find water in this nightmarish place to wash her wounds.

She needed to get out as fast as she could. She took a tentative step forward. Without warning, a sob pressed its way up her throat and burst out of her with such intensity it added to her fear. The tears flowed endlessly. She took two more steps. The earth crunched beneath her. More tears. Two more steps. A chill snaked through her. Tears.

A tickle on her ear stopped her forward motion. What was that? A spider web? She jerked her hand frantically and swiped at her ear. Her frenzied pulse increased. She could still feel the gentle touch, like a down feather caressing her ear. Not a spider web. She couldn't wipe it away.

One more step. "I'll either have to sit here in the dark and die or walk this alone, I guess." Her voice was sharp enough to cut glass. She grit her teeth and inhaled deeply. She ventured a couple more steps. Was that pressure on her back again? "Are you there?" The tickle on her ear continued.

A couple of more steps. Then several more. Was she actually doing this? Head held high, she walked forward for several steps. The fear seemed to dissipate. But, after a while her legs became heavy and weak and her mouth dry as sawdust. She stopped abruptly and sat. How much longer? A strong wind blew past her, stinging her face with debris. Her trembling hands covered her face and she wept. Will this journey ever end? She wallowed in the dirt and moaned.

Was that pressure on her back, again? She jerked herself up. She didn't want to feel this. She just wanted to get out of this tunnel. But her feet seemed determined not to move. Warmth embraced her fingertips. She balled her hands into a fist and pulled them to her chest. Fear that had been in remission, returned. Warmth enveloped her elbow. She jerked her arm forward. She needed to get out of this place. She took a step and another and another. The effort was taxing. Her head hung low on her stooped shoulders. She was cold and tired. Loneliness and fear squeezed her like a vice. Bent and broken, her tears resurfaced.

She dragged her feet forward, scraping them across the dirt, kicking up dust. She coughed and covered her nose. She could feel the grime on her cheeks.

Overwhelmed, she covered her face and wailed. She never should have started on this trip. She could be out there with everyone else if she hadn't made a commitment to this journey. Why had she done it? Now she was alone, frightened and angry. Where was the love? The companionship? The promises?

She collapsed to her knees and slumped forward, unable to go further. With her face buried in her arms on the cold earth, she shivered alone in the dark. Fear and grief crept from her gut, and she called out into the eternal blackness. "Why did you leave me? You told me you would never leave me, you would keep me safe." She groaned through her misery and tears. "I hate you for leaving me." She whimpered with pain, then in a relenting whisper, "I just want this to end. I just want to die." *Why couldn't things be like they were before this black tunnel consumed me?* Her agony fed on what little hope remained in her heart. She stayed crumpled there a long time.

Gentle warmth settled on her back. Her tears paused. Now what? She lifted her head high enough to peek up. The tunnel was flooded with light. She bolted up and surveyed the area. She saw him just in front of her, his arms stretched wide, welcoming her.

"Where have you been? You said you wouldn't leave me." The words shot out between grinding teeth. She choked and wept.

"I never did." He gestured for her to look behind her.

She turned and her jaw fell as her eyes grazed each scene. The tunnel was illuminated all the way to the entrance. Her gasp echoed, bouncing off the tunnel walls.

She stared. Her journey displayed before her like tiny vignettes from a Hollywood movie. He was present in each, protecting her from the dangerous people loitering in the tunnel's dark crevices. He steered her clear of deep potholes on the road and pulled her away from fissures filled with vermin. Wild animals growled and snapped but remained in the crags, unable to draw near to her. He was a shield covering her, keeping them all at bay.

Unable to speak, she turned back to him, her jaw still lax, and gazed up. Warmth pushed up from her toes, through her legs. Her fingers tingled with feeling, and the warmth continued up her wrists to her shoulders, to her chest, and settled in her heart.

He nodded. "My banner over you is love. You left me, but I never left you."

She lowered her eyes, and dropped her head. She caught sight of her hands. They were clean. She stood and checked her knees. The abrasions were healed, the blood gone. She touched her face. The grime was gone. She assessed her whole body. It was spotless. Not a glimpse of dirt. She lifted her eyes to him struggling to find words.

"Forgive me for doubting you, for hating you." Her voice broke.

He reached his hand to her. She tried to take it, but hesitated. She took one tiny step forward and he rushed to her and embraced her.

"Of course, I forgive you. Because I love you. I always have and I always will."

1Kings 19:11-13

Mary A. Allen lives with her husband in the Sacramento area. She works as a Home Health nurse and writes in her spare time. Her first novel, **Crying in the Morgue, Laughing in the Dark** *is a fictionalized account of the first part of her journey. And, her journey continues.*

GOD'S LOVE

Heather D. Blackman

The love of God.
A love so incomparable,
It cannot be earned,
It cannot be lost.
Your love is unconditional
To the loveable and the unlovable,
The obedient and the rebellious.
A love so profound,
It is without borders,
Spanning beyond the universe,
Transcending the limits of my mind.
A love so pure,
It exemplifies perfection.
Your love never fails or disappoints.
You are the Creator of Love.
I was created to love You,
Created to be loved by You.

Heather D. Blackman is honored to share her creative spirit through her passion for writing poetry. Her poems have been published in **Inspire Promise**, **Inspire Forgiveness,** *and* **Inspire Joy**. *It is Heather's desire that her poetry will uplift, encourage, and express the love of our Heavenly Father.*

THE BEST CHOICE

Margaret Lalich

I believe love is a choice and that love is the most wondrous, soul satisfying, and worthwhile thing a human being can engage in. At different times in my life, love has been fun, peaceful, scary, joyous, exciting, painful, comforting, effortless, or simply hard work. In hard times, it's been a determined, deliberate, conscious, choice that must be made minute-by-minute, hourly, and daily, and it is the best choice we can make. It's a gift, and a command.

If you keep My commandments, you will abide in My love, just as I have kept My Father's commandments and abide in His love. These things I have spoken to you, that My joy may remain in you, and that your joy may be full. This is My commandment, that you love one another as I have loved you. (John 15:10-12 NKJV)

Medical research has confirmed that love is good for your heart. Romantic love, family love, or love for our fellow man is a sweetheart deal that's all good. Love has nothing to do with sugar-laden, heart-shaped goodies, and is not fattening.

Maybe you have found, as I have, that living out your love (through hard times), can be a challenge. It's not always a sweet, and gooey, chocolate experience. Just as too much sugar isn't good for us, and melted chocolate can be messy, maybe a little occasional sauerkraut is good too.

Some proclaim that love and hate are flip sides of the same coin. I disagree. Without a doubt, both are strong emotions. But I think that's where the similarity ends. Hate seeks to hurt, diminish, or destroy its target, while love seeks to magnify its ultimate good. This seems a perfect contradiction. How can it be that something so sublime and perfect (love) is often wrapped in so much of the opposite *stuff*?

Psychological research says we can't engage two opposing emotions at the same time. In fact, one strategy for changing a troubled mind is to deliberately focus on an opposite feeling. But we *can* love a person, and hate their behavior or circumstance at the same time. That's a different story.

Scripture says the mouth speaks out of the abundance of the *heart*, and that we can't draw sweet water from a bitter well. Blessing and cursing each express strong feelings, but we are cautioned about offering both. (Matthew 12:34, James 3:10-12 NKJV)

Can sweet water be contaminated? Yes. I've seen that, and I bet you have too. Some circumstances provoke overwhelming challenge. Bitterness may be a result. Sweet words left unspoken, or bitter ones shared in the face of continued stress, fatigue, worry, complaints, or serious illness, are contaminants. Feeling ignored, under-appreciated, or defeated when we try and fail to make things better, is also painful. All of those can be toxic.

The *choice* to love serves as a filter, and a shield to help protect the heart from lasting damage. By itself, the deliberate *act* of choosing love reduces pollution, and helps to clear the emotional environment. It's hard sometimes—but always powerful.

Physical and mental pain can make a person irritable, inconsolable, and frustrated. In this state, some lash out, not aiming to hit the ones they love, but often doing so, because our nearest and dearest folks are the ones standing by…within striking distance. Like lightning rods, loved ones often seem to draw fire. It hurts. Those things may not destroy love—but they can force renewal of the *choice*, again and again.

Sometimes love burns bright, like fireworks streaking into the heavens. Sometimes, instead, it glows as a burning ember, or a flickering candle. *Always* it is a light of life, even in dark times. Did you know the light of a single candle is visible in darkness, to the naked eye, at a distance of a mile or more? In fact, the darker the environment—the brighter even the smallest light appears. To keep our emotional candles glowing, we hold on, deliberately recalling the qualities of our "first-love." We strike a new match with every choice we make to recall or to seek "whatsoever things are lovely." (Philippians 4:8 NKJV)

Take courage because there *are* lovely things to be found, when we carefully seek them. We can choose to have a treasure hunt, by candlelight. Each time we choose to love (no matter what)… our bond becomes stronger, richer, deeper, and more worthy of constant, conscious, choosing. This is real and lasting treasure.

Scripture reminds us:

Love suffers long and is kind; love does not envy; love does not parade itself, is not puffed up; does not behave rudely, does not seek its own, is not provoked, thinks no evil; does not rejoice in iniquity, but rejoices in the truth; bears all things, believes all things, hopes all things, endures all things. (I Corinthians 13: 4-6 NKJV)

Physical and mental illness can call for that kind of endurance. Watching my dear one battle his depression/anxiety disorder, and his physical difficulties, gave me a whole new appreciation for his challenge. He lived courageously through daily struggles, with as much wit and grace as he could muster. Lightning did strike, more than once, yet we were still standing together as the storms eased.

Those who face personal crises, and persist through, this kind of challenge deserve a medal of honor. Maybe we should design a special type of "purple heart" to recognize both visible and invisible wounds. Maybe such medals would help us recall bravery under fire, and stir up more love for our heroes.

Choosing love, no matter what, can be a heavy investment. It also pays rich dividends. Take a deep breath, hold hands, and seek. Moments of peace and laughter still exist in the midst of it all. We can find them together and, when we do, those moments deserve to be recognized and joyously *celebrated*.

My husband was my best friend, partner, playmate and lover for forty-five years before he died. He fought hard to keep his balance in the last several of those years, as his independence, comfort, and peace of mind became increasingly rare. He was, and still is, my hero. We laughed. We cried. We prayed, and we were blessed. I heard a phrase that seems to fit our experience. It sounds like it belongs in a good ole' country song. "Even the bad times are good." They were, and I miss them.

If you are going through a dark time right now, I pray you will find strength and comfort knowing that you are not alone.

May you find sweet water for your thirsty heart, and may you find courage in knowing that "tears may fill the night, but joy comes in the morning" (Psalms 30:5 NKJV). Don't be afraid to reach out for help, and the support of others who love *you*.

Love is what makes the world go around, and makes it worth taking the spin...even with occasional dizziness. Love can be fierce. It can be *fun*. And it can be forever. Now, if we could just wrap it up in non-fattening chocolate, nuts, and marshmallows, our "rocky roads" could be even more delicious.

Knowing the delight we find in our Lord, and the delight that He takes in us, is better than whipped cream or any other treat. Paul wrote a beautiful and encouraging summation:

Neither height, nor depth, nor anything else in all creation, will be able to separate us from the love of God that is in Christ Jesus our Lord. (Romans 8:39 NKJV)

Margaret Lalich is a believer, a lover (family, friends and others), a relentless optimist, and a Certified Laughter Leader. She is also a writer and teacher. At 73 years young, she is a mom, grandma, great grandmother...and widow of Joseph Lalich, who was the love of her life.

WHEN GOD FEELS HIDDEN
Deb Gruelle

All night long on my bed I looked for the one my heart loves;
I looked for him but did not find him.

(Song of Songs 3:1)

I've had times when my heart danced because I felt so close to God. In other dark seasons, through long stretches of time when God's only response to my intense prayers was silence, I've felt a vast canyon between God and me. For instance, during the six years I prayed to have our first baby, I struggled with whether God had withdrawn from me. Did God love me less during this time?

Other believers throughout history confirm that they've also experienced these seasons of God withdrawing the awareness of His presence from them too. Why would a loving God allow this just when we need the awareness of His presence most?

Through my seasons of feeling God's distance, I've come to believe that God does this to draw our hearts toward Him in a new way. I now see these dark seasons as times of divine instruction, drawing me out of complacency to seek a new, deeper way of leaning into Him. When I connected with God on such a deep level that I came to depend on the awareness of His presence, I began to focus on the wonderful goal of feeling good in God's presence. To save me from the mistaken impression that I'd always feel good when following God, He strengthened me to walk by faith, not by experience. God gently removes my fingers from grasping only a shadow of truth, of learning to depend on the feeling of His presence.

Because God is always for us, He wants to train us to seek Him at a deeper level than we were capable of earlier. When our feeling of connection and living close to God is removed for a season, it's natural for confusion and feeling forgotten to be our first reactions, but in the wrestling, our resolve to listen to His truth strengthens. Satan tries to convince us during these times that God doesn't care about what is happening to us, and depression can creep in when we no longer feel close to Jesus, but we must not mistake His mysterious workings for rejection.

What do we do in times of darkness or distance? We hold onto God's character and His truthful Word that He'll never leave us. We remember that God is trustworthy, faithful, and loves us to pieces. We trust Him even when we don't understand. We continue to seek Him in the dark, even when we don't feel Him. When we come through on the bright side of a long, dark season, we recognize more deeply that God alone is enough.

For me, I needed my faith to be strengthened deep inside to weather the total of seventeen years it would take to complete our family. I learned that God was with me each step of the way whether I felt Him or not.

Prayer: *Father, thank You that Your Word is true no matter how we feel. Thank You so much that Your love doesn't depend on whether* we can drum up feelings of Your love. During our dark seasons, help us see glimpses of You to encourage us to keep walking in truth.

*Deb Gruelle, a new Inspire member, has been writing for over two decades. Because she had so much trouble getting her kids to go to sleep, she wrote a picture book, **Ten Little Night Stars** (release date is January, 2018). She also wrote **The Ache for a Child**, for women dealing with infertility.*

Love Said…

Tessa Burns

I will hold your hand as you go on your way.

I will be right next to you in dark places.

I will stretch my arms wide for you as you
spit in My face.

I will look you in the eye with compassion as
you deny you even know Me.

And after you have walked away,

I will seek you and find you.

Enfolding you in My arms as you hang your
head in shame.

And just as the dawn arises anew each day,

I will reveal the same is true for you.

I will gently embrace your chin, lift your
head, look in your eyes and remind you;

You are redeemed,

You are valuable,

You are My prize,

You are loved with an everlasting love.

Tessa lives in Northern California with her husband and three grown children. Her hope as she journeys through life is to encourage others to notice the beauty all around them and inside of them, and to understand and know how deeply they are loved.

Sessions of Love

Julie Blackman

Archie Mulligan was a creature of habit. Every day at noon, he sat at a table and ate the same thing: a turkey sandwich with avocado, mayonnaise, lettuce, and tomato on whole-wheat bread. For dessert, he had a shiny red apple along with a sixteen-ounce bottle of water.

Archie worked as an office janitor and had a sweet disposition. His co-worker, Michelle, guessed him to be in his late sixties or early seventies, but she wasn't sure. She figured he was just short of five feet nine, somewhat on the thin side, and with the darkest brown eyes she'd ever seen. When people said, "the eyes are the window to the soul," they were right. When he looked at a person, they felt like they were facing pure love. Instead of being a man filled with pride or insincerity, he was kind and generous. Before lunch, he'd say a quick prayer, clap his hands, rub them together, then take a big bite out of his sandwich. A big smile would follow, then a nod. "My wife did it again, Michelle!"

It was a treat to watch Archie talk with people during lunch. The entire office looked to him as the company's Grandfather of Wisdom. If people had a problem, they went to Archie. He always knew what to say, or he'd ask a question which helped them figure things out on their own. And somehow, he always found a way to talk about God. Michelle, who had lunch with him frequently, teased him all the time, and told him he should have been a psychotherapist or psychiatrist. However, everyone felt grateful he wasn't.

"I'm so glad that he isn't a therapist or I couldn't afford these sessions. Don't you see that we're getting free counseling?" remarked Amanda, the company receptionist.

Today, Della, the company accountant, spoke with Archie. With her boisterous personality, she didn't care who heard what they were talking about. She amused him with stories about her grandchildren and shared how her kids struggled when she tried to instill discipline. "In my day, Archie, I could never get away with what they do today. You just have to put your foot down and not let them run the show. How are they going to turn out when they get older? I keep warning my daughter, but it falls on deaf ears."

As usual, with his calm demeanor, Archie shared some words of wisdom that did the trick. Della jumped out of her seat and threw her arms around him. "Oh Archie, that's why I come to you. You always have a perspective I haven't thought about. That's a great idea. Thanks! I'm going to call my daughter right now." Della grabbed her lunch bag and scurried out of the break room.

❧

The next day, Michelle could tell that Archie didn't seem like his usual self. But, he still met with Amanda who was crying.

Unlike Della, who loved to hear herself speak and made sure everyone else heard what she was saying, Amanda talked softly. Everyone in the office respected Archie. And whenever he was in one of his "sessions" with another employee, it was an unwritten code: Give employees and Archie their privacy. The office only consisted of ten people, so they functioned more like a family rather than a business.

Michelle watched as Archie leaned in closer to talk to Amanda. He didn't take a bite of his sandwich until after he finished talking with her. *There's just something different about this man, and I can't put my finger on it. I don't think I've ever met anyone like him.* Someone in the break room started coughing, and Michelle looked to her right to see Frank, the head of facilities, shaking his head at her. *Oops!* She'd been caught staring at Archie in a session again. Mouthing "sorry" to Frank, Michelle picked up her mystery novel and began reading.

Amanda got up and walked out of the room. Michelle glanced over and saw Archie wiping his sweaty brow. "Hey, Archie, are you okay?"

"Michelle, I think I may be coming down with something. Oh boy, I'm gonna be in trouble with the wife. She told me to get my flu shot a long time ago, but I put it off until two weeks ago. I've probably caught something."

"Why don't you go home and get some rest. You know we can't make it here without you."

"Yes, Archie, get out of here. I meant to tell you to leave early," Frank said.

Michelle helped Archie pack up his lunch and gather his belongings, and then walked alongside him to his car. "Will you be okay getting home?" Michelle asked.

"Hey, Michelle!" Frank shouted. "Follow him home."

"Okay, let me get my purse and car keys."

Archie's house was only a few minutes away from the office, but Michelle was glad she followed him. He needed help getting out of his car and walking up to the house. Michelle held onto him as she rang the doorbell. Agnes, his wife, opened the door.

"I knew Archie shouldn't have gone to work today," Agnes said. "Thank you so much, Michelle. Come in and I'll fix you some tea."

"I'd love to, but I have to get back to work. Frank wanted me to make sure Archie got home safely. He seems quite weak. I think you may have to call the doctor." For the first time, Michelle felt concerned and asked Agnes, "If it isn't too much trouble, would you mind giving me a call later to let me know how he's doing?"

"Yes, but please come in for a moment. It's so nice to have people like you who care."

"Mrs. Mulligan, you have no idea how much all of us at the office love Archie. We've nicknamed him our Grandfather of Wisdom."

Agnes smiled and led Michelle to the living room and motioned for her to have a seat. "Let me get Archie settled and I'll be right back." After twenty minutes, Agnes returned. "I just called the doctor's office, and he's going to stop by this afternoon. We're so blessed that he makes house calls. I can't thank you enough for taking the time to follow Archie home. That was a sweet gesture."

"You're very welcome. If he doesn't come back to work this week, may I have your telephone number to call you over the weekend to see how he's doing? Here's my cell phone number."

"Of course," replied Agnes. Her eyes lit up.

৩

Over the next few days, it wasn't the same around the office without Archie. Everyone could feel it. When the weekend finally arrived, Michelle couldn't wait to get an update from Agnes. She reached for her phone and dialed his home number. "Hi Agnes, this is Michelle from Archie's office."

"Hello dear. How are you?"

"I'm fine. How's the patient? Frank mentioned that Archie has a cold?"

"Yes, it's nothing too serious, but I wasn't risking him going to work."

"If he's up to it, may I speak to him?"

"Sure, hold on."

"Hello?" Archie said in a weak voice.

"Hi Archie, this is, Michelle. I wanted to check in and see how you're doing."

"I'm doing all right. My wife keeps asking me why I won't retire. But I tell her I love interacting with young people. They keep me young. I should be back next week. By the way, thanks for the card."

"You're welcome. I had everyone sign it."

"So many kind words. I had no idea I meant that much to everyone. I thought you all were just humoring an old man and keeping me company during lunch."

"I don't think you realize how very important you are to us, Archie, and how much you're loved. I haven't been eavesdropping, but I've watched how you encourage, comfort, and show kindness to those who look to you, and there was something so familiar about your actions. At first, I couldn't put my finger on it. Then it dawned on me. I remembered a Scripture my grandmother used to recite to me when I was a little girl.

"'Love is patient, love is kind. It does not envy, it does not boast, it is not proud. It does not dishonor others, it is not self-seeking, it is not easily angered, it keeps no record of wrongs. Love does not delight in evil but rejoices with the truth. It always protects, always trusts, always hopes, always perseveres (1 Corinthians 13:4-7).'

"Archie, this is you! This is the type of love I see you demonstrate to all of us in the office. Get well soon, we miss you. Oh, and when you get back, I need to book another session."

Julie Blackman writes fiction short stories and nonfiction inspirational pieces. She thinks words are precious and the biggest loss is to not share them. She considers writing a privilege and desires to be a writing instrument for God. Her work is published in **Inspire Victory, Inspire Promise, Inspire Forgiveness,** *and* **Inspire Joy.**

PERFECT LOVE

Guadalupe C. Casillas

Have you ever been loved with "perfect" love by another human being? Has a spouse, friend, parent, or your children been capable of loving you unconditionally? Can you rely on someone to be one hundred percent good and faithful to you, even in their thoughts? Only a perfect Heavenly Father can love you like that.

First, let's look at the dictionary's definition of *perfect* and *love*.

perfect:

1a: being entirely without fault or defect: flawless;
1b: satisfying all requirements: accurate

love:

1a: strong affection for another arising out of kinship or personal ties; 1b: affection based on admiration, benevolence, or common interests

2: an assurance of love

God is love. I can say I love someone, but I can't say, "I am love." Only God can.

I attended a Christian workshop about loving our husbands. The speaker asked us to make a list of reasons why we love our husbands and fill in the blank:

I love my husband because _____.

The reasons mentioned were: He is a good provider, listens to me, helps me around the house, he's a good father, makes me laugh, he's caring and loving, responsible...and so forth.

We were surprised when the speaker said, "Did you notice your list was conditional? Would you love your husband if he wasn't responsible? What if he doesn't help you around the house? What if he's an alcoholic or workaholic?"

We love when our spouses meet our physical and emotional needs. We're content when they treat us well. But true love is unconditional and at times sacrificial...ouch! We were reminded of our wedding vows—for better or for worse.

Only God's love is perfect. He loves us even with our imperfections. We have right standing with God, in spite of our shortcomings, because of Jesus' sacrifice on the cross. God is patient with us. He forgives us repeatedly and takes the time to correct us.

Whether single or married we desire to be loved and accepted at all times. But in this world, we'll suffer rejection and disappointments. At times, you might feel unloved by a friend or a relative. Keep in mind that God, your Creator, loves you unconditionally and He'll never leave you nor forsake you. He loves you so much, that in order to prove His love for you, He chose to give up His life—that is love!

For years I searched for unconditional love. Even though my husband and I love each other, we have hurt each other's feelings when we acted selfishly. At times, I sought Eduardo's love and attention but a soccer game seemed more important to him. Other times, I was extra sensitive and became easily hurt by careless words. We have overcome some of those issues by scheduling times to talk without distractions. I can let him enjoy his game without interruptions, unless it can't wait. When our scheduled time arrives, we enjoy our conversation.

As a newlywed, I wanted my husband to meet all my needs and give me his unconditional love all the time. I wasn't aware Eduardo had become my "god." He was number one in my heart. If he was charming, I was happy. If he spent more time watching sports on TV than talking to me, I felt rejected. My world revolved around him. Can you relate to this? It doesn't only happen to women. Men can also feel neglected when their wives place other priorities ahead of them. Do you realize seeking the approval of our spouses more than God's, is a result of when sin entered the world?

This was one of the curses: "Your desire will be for your husband." Prior to this, Eve's desire may have been for God first.

When my husband and I argued, I couldn't believe the person I loved could hurt my feelings and not seem to care. I never forgot the words of wisdom God gave me through my sister-in-law, "My brother is imperfect and just a human being. The only one who can ever satisfy all of your deepest needs is Jesus." She was right. Slowly, I realized my husband, as much as he loves me, was not capable of loving me the way God does.

From that moment on, whenever I was hurt, I prayed, "Thank you, Lord, that You listen to me all the time. You're always here for me and love me unconditionally." I didn't need to make an appointment to speak to God. He was the only One fully capable of healing my hurts.

Through the years I grew to love God with all my heart. He became number one. When I told my husband he was number two in my life because God had taken the number one place, he smiled and said, "I like being number two—it's too much pressure being number one." My husband was glad I found the One who could satisfy all my needs.

My two sons constantly reassure me of their love and appreciation. We have many wonderful memories. But I couldn't find "perfect love" in my children either. When my sons became teenagers, they valued the opinions of their peers more, and would even be embarrassed to be seen with my husband and me by their friends. Even though this is a natural process when they're this age, I was somewhat hurt. I thought of all the sleepless nights I sacrificed when they were babies. I said, "Lord, I'm convinced You are the only One who can love me with a perfect love."

You've probably been hurt by those close to you. This doesn't mean you can't love or trust the people around you, but the only One who'll never disappoint you is the One who carried your sins and died for you on the cross.

❦

Guadalupe loves to lead Bible studies and is currently a Speaker for Stonecroft Ministries.
Her Bible study, **How to Love God with All Your Heart - A Personal Journey & Testimonial Bible Study Guide** *is now available on Amazon.*

Excerpt from *How to Love God with All Your Heart – A Personal Journey & Testimonial Bible Study Guide* by Guadalupe C. Casillas © 2015

OF LOVE, VINES, AND VALENTINES

Sandra Fischer

For His lovingkindness is great toward us,
And the truth of the LORD is everlasting.

Praise the LORD! (Psalm 117:2 NASB)

Have you ever noticed how the vines on a Mandevilla or Clematis plant intertwine so tightly that you can't distinguish one from another? It occurs to me this expresses the word "lovingkindness" which appears many times in the Book of Psalms. The compounding of these two benevolent actions make them truly inseparable—one can't be sincerely kind without loving nor truly loving without being kind. The essence of the one is inexorably intertwined with that of the other.

Each year we celebrate Valentine's Day with its various expressions of love and kindness. While the St. Valentine tradition of sending love messages is a good one, I like what another saint named Augustine said:

"What does Love look like? It has hands to help others. It has feet to hasten to the poor and needy. It has eyes to see misery and want. It has ears to hear the sighs and sorrows of fellow men. That is what Love looks like."

In Augustine's view, love is manifested through our deepest sensitivity to others' needs, followed by putting that love into sacrificial action. This is lovingkindness. You can see it in those who aid victims of natural disasters, such as wildfires, mudslides, and devastating hurricanes.

We don't have to go far to find it in our own backyards—neighbors and friends reaching out to those suffering from a disabling disease, the loss of a loved one, or other heartbreaks, those personal "Tsunamis" and "mudslides" that overwhelm us. "Each man's grief is my own," a line from the '50s song, "No Man Is an Island" from John Donne's reflection, captures the whole idea of how our lives are intertwined.

God spread His lovingkindness abroad as an example of what our relationship should be with Him and with others. We need Him. We need each other. We need lovingkindness. Perhaps that's why the Master Gardener "planted" the idea in the first place.

"Father, help us to be so wrapped in Your lovingkindness that our hearts will intertwine with others to demonstrate its everlasting beauty."

*Sandra Fischer taught high school English and owned a Christian bookstore in Indiana before retiring and devoting time to writing. Many of her stories and articles are gleaned from her experiences growing up in the Midwest. She is the author of the book, **Seasons in the Garden.***

Excerpt from *Seasons in the Garden*, Evergood Books, 2015

Unique Love

Ani Avdalyan

A unique type of love that can't be replaced,
It sticks with you like a strong paste,
Even though you can't really see it,
Without a doubt, you can feel it.

When you are loved,
It's the opposite of being shoved,
It feels like you are beloved,
Something you have always dreamed of.

So, you see it's a type of love,
That comes from above,
The love of God it is,
And a strong power of His.

His love is stronger than anything,
It will want to make you sing,
Even if you're upset,
It will never be a threat.

For you are guarded by the Lord,
With the Angels' mighty sword,
God is always with you,
I hope you believe it's true.

God's love is all throughout the Bible,
The book that is really reliable,
His love makes you roar,
Because He's waiting for you at the door.

Ani attends a Christian school in Northern California and likes to spend her time by using her thoughts and creativity on writing books. Ani also likes to get inspiration by readig many books. She's planning on using her writing to remind people about who God is and what He did.

ANN'S CHRISTMAS

Judy Pierce

The choir was singing "O Come All Ye Faithful," as Ann walked into the century old church. The ceiling was high and open, stained glass windows lined the sides and front of the beautiful building, and wooden pews were overflowing with families smiling and wishing each other Merry Christmas. She saw Beth standing and waving at her from the front of the sanctuary. Ann waved back and weaved through the crowded center aisle to her friend. As she made her way through the crowd, she noticed that the end of each pew was decorated with a pretty wreath. The old traditional church was trimmed with wreaths, garlands, holly, and white candles. A life-sized crèche stood to the right of the podium.

Ann looked up at the large stained-glass window located at the front of the church depicting Jesus standing at a door and knocking. She had memorized Rev. 3:20 (NASB), "Behold, I stand at the door and knock; if anyone hears My voice and opens the door, I will come in to him, and will dine with him, and he with Me." The scene and scripture were among the many reasons she felt at home here.

She smiled as she came to a stop beside Beth. "We've been watching for you," said her friend as they hugged. "We saved you a seat. You know how crowded the Christmas service is."

They slid into the pew next to Beth's husband John, and teenagers Brittany and David. "Thank you, Beth. Merry Christmas everyone."

"Merry Christmas Ann," the family replied in unison.

"We are so glad you agreed to spend the day with us," said Beth. "Doesn't the church look beautiful? The wreaths on the end of the pews are a nice touch, and look at the crèche. It's breathtaking."

"Yes, and the music too," said Ann. "I enjoy listening to our choir sing Christmas carols. 'Silent Night' is my favorite but I love them all."

The church quieted as Reverend Dearborn appeared and walked to the podium. He was dressed in a tailored dark blue suit and his familiar red Christmas tie. He had worn the same tie for several years, a gift from his wife Laura.

Ann listened as the tall, gray-haired man said, "Good morning," in an uplifting voice. "Welcome to this wondrous day, the celebration of our Lord Jesus' birth." He preached a sermon about the birth of Jesus and quoted, "The angels came to the shepherds and said, "Do not be afraid. I bring you good news of great joy that will be for all the people. Today in the town of David a savior has been born to you; he is Christ the Lord." He added, "This is the heart of Christmas. God loved us enough to send his only begotten Son so that we might live through him."

Love, hope, joy, and salvation are what Christmas means to me, thought Ann. *They are part of the foundation for my faith. The last few years have tested and strengthened it.*

Ann's mind wandered as the choir began singing. *It has been four years since Kevin died. He was tired, but we didn't realize anything was wrong. Tired was the warning sign but how often in life is that a death sentence? His job was demanding and he was working all those hours of overtime. The heart attack happened so fast, my wonderful husband gone in minutes. I miss him every day. I know I should be grateful and content with everything I have and for the generous people in my life but, God, I need your help to let go and your guidance to find my way.*

"Ave Maria" brought Ann back to the present. Beautiful music filled the church and Ann with a sense of peace. She closed her eyes and surrendered. *Not my will, but Thine be done.*

Reverend Dearborn concluded the service with a final amen. The choir sang "Joy to the World," as the congregation stood and began the slow process of emptying the church. Ann and her friends visited and hugged their way out of the building. Many people shared they were on their way to cozy Christmas celebrations with family and friends, while others were on their way to volunteer feeding the less fortunate Christmas dinner.

"Will you miss volunteering this year, Ann?" asked Beth.

"Yes and no," said Ann. "Preparing and serving dinner to the homeless was rewarding, and I plan to do it again. But this year I'm looking forward to spending the day with you and John and the kids. I guess they aren't kids anymore. It will be fun to watch them unwrap their gifts, and I'm looking forward to turkey, dressing, and cranberry sauce. I'm so glad you included me."

"All of us are too. We think of you as family, you know. Time to go, I have a turkey that needs attention."

cↄ

Ann helped Beth prepare the feast as they laughed and shared Christmas stories. They had met and become friends during third grade. The close friendship had expanded to four when they met Kevin and John during high school. John interjected his memories into the conversation, while Brittany and David listened and asked questions. They added a few stories too.

"Talking about Kevin today is healing," said Ann. "He is here with us through our stories. I'm learning to let go, but Kevin will always be in my heart."

A kitchen timer sounded signaling the turkey was ready to come out of the oven. As the oven door opened, the tantalizing smell seeped out into the kitchen and dining room. Rolls were placed in the oven to warm, while the dressing, corn, and mashed potatoes were placed in serving dishes. The whir of the electric knife signaled the carving of the turkey and that dinner was almost ready.

"Dinner is served," said Ann, surveying the trays and dishes of hot food. "Hours of work for a meal that will be gone in minutes."

They sat down at the dinner table, covered in an ivory tablecloth. The table was set with sparkling Lennox China and silverware that were used for special occasions. Two candles twinkled as John said grace. When he was done, Ann said, "I'd like to add a quote from Mother Teresa. "Let no one ever come to you without leaving better and happier. Be the living expression of God's kindness: kindness in your face, kindness in your eyes, kindness in your smile." She looked at her friends and added, "This is your gift to me today."

The rest of the afternoon was filled with delicious food, gifts, conversation, and washing dishes. When it was time to drive home, Ann was given generous portions of turkey and several side dishes to eat the following day. She also kept her promise to call when she arrived home.

"I am grateful for this day," she said as she slipped on her nightgown and began evening prayers. "I am grateful for my friends who gave me the gift of belonging and sharing, and for my church and Reverend Dearborn's sermon and the choir. I am grateful for the time and love Kevin and I shared. Because of him I have known unconditional love and believe that it can happen again in my life. Most of all, I am grateful to God."

Ann opened her Bible to 1 John 4:7-8: "Beloved, let us love one another, because love comes from God. Everyone who loves has been born of God and knows God. The one who does not love does not know God, for God is love."

She closed the Bible reflected on the message. *This is the first day I have felt unconditional love in four years. It has been a Merry Christmas indeed.*

Judy Ann Pierce enjoys writing stories that entertain and enable her readers. Judy advocates kindness for all people and animals. Gratitude is a daily practice that strengthens her faith. She lives in Northern California with her husband, Larry, and their horses, cats, and corgis. www. judyannpierce.com

Secret of a Happy Marriage

Janet Ann Collins

My husband and I were in our late 20s when we got engaged.

We chose and approached several "old" (in their 40s and 50s) couples in our church who had relationships we admired. They weren't all kissy and romantic, but seemed to have strong bonds and to care deeply about each other.

We wanted to ask them for advice in having a happy marriage like theirs, so we asked each couple if we could visit them. All of them agreed to meet with us and arranged times when we could chat together.

But every time when we arrived and told them why we had come, they were amazed and said, "We can't believe you chose us! We almost got divorced!"

Then they told us about difficult times in their marriages. Some had gotten counseling, while others had handled their problems on their own with prayer and effort, but they had all worked through them.

It was obvious to us that their relationships had become stronger as a result. So, we got married, knowing that if there were difficult times it would make our marriage stronger to work through the problems.

And we certainly had plenty of opportunities to do that. Some of the things we dealt with were kids with special needs, long periods of unemployment and economic problems, chronic illness, and so much more.

But, by the grace of God, we dealt with all of them and had a strong and loving relationship until death did us part.

Marriages are not all kisses and love songs. Sometimes they are hard work. But, trusting God, the struggles make everything that comes after so much sweeter.

Janet Ann Collins is an author of several books for kids, and her work has been published in many anthologies and periodicals. She's also a public speaker, teacher, and grandmother.

Diamonds in the Rough

Michelle Van Vliet

I have a confession. I used to be an eBay vendor. Yep, It's true. I love garage sales, flea markets, and old dusty treasures that most people would rather discard. To me, they are "diamonds in the rough," and I find it crazy-satisfying when others see value in those nostalgic-somethings too. I guess that's why selling on eBay was a good fit for me back in the day. I sold everything from old Champion™ juicers, to toy tractors, and old hats. It was fun to find a diamond in the rough and give it another chance at life. It was usually a bit of a gamble too, because no matter what I originally paid, the real value was always determined by the highest bid at the end of the auction.

I remember the day I picked up two old dusty boxes of Barbie dolls at a garage sale. My husband must have thought I was crazy since I spent about all we had left in our budget. I had no idea what was in the boxes, but I handed the man $25, piled them in my car, and drove away with a new treasure.

That night, as I unpacked the boxes, I took my first look at the mess before me. It was hideous. A Ken doll with chewed up legs and a missing arm, a Barbie head with no body, dolls I didn't recognize, and old clothes and accessories that seemed worthless. It didn't help that my husband sat three feet away from me, as I scrubbed layers of dirt off those old things for who knows how long. He probably wondered why he married such a crazy person. I remember wishing I had waited until he was at work so I could hide the grime of my purchase. But sometimes Barbies hold intrinsic value. Maybe there was value hidden underneath the dirt and grime.

As I scrubbed, the pressure got to me. When I found a pair of small red shoes requiring no cleaning, I took a picture, went to the computer, and listed them on the spot. In my hurry I accidentally added an extra zero to the starting bid. I realized immediately what I did and went back to change the amount from $20 to $2. However, I was shocked they were already purchased. Apparently, if the bottom image says, "Made in Japan," it's a big deal. Who knew a tiny pair of red plastic shoes would sell for more than what I paid for the real pair sitting in my closet? With new wind in my sails, I listed a few more things. The Barbie without a body sold for $52. And that chewed-up Ken doll? Someone purchased him for $73. Clothes were sold by the outfit for over $150, cars and Francie dolls for even more. (Turns out, the dolls I didn't recognize were Francie and Midge, also a big deal.) In the end, my little investment of twenty-five "junkie" dollars turned into over $2,500!

To most people, the contents of those boxes weren't diamonds in the rough. They looked more like old, dirty, discarded junk. I had no idea what they were worth until I knew what someone was willing to pay for them. The people who bought them understood their real value.

And that's my story. It's your story too. For God SO LOVED [emphasis added] the world that He gave his one and only Son…(John 3:16). He became the highest bidder.

Like the dusty treasures I used to find on eBay, we are diamonds in the rough. Each of us holds intrinsic beauty and value that come from being His. But, much like what I found in those boxes, we may look at our lives and see all the mess and blemishes and devalue our worth. Sometimes the pressure gets to us, as we try to scrub out blemishes by acting like someone who has it all together. We hide, like I wanted to hide the dirty boxes from my husband. There is something more profound than your muck, however.

In your messiest condition, someone saw you and wanted you. He is the one who sits with you in the mess and lovingly tends to your dusty story, redeeming it for something beautiful. You were made in His image. Your value was determined on the cross. Your potential has resurrection power.

Even when the dust and grime of our circumstances, or the broken ways in which we live, shroud us, God finds crazy joy in redeeming our story. The deeper our honesty about it, the more deeply we will know and experience Him. When His love infuses the chapters of our story, those chapters become redeemed. The apostle Paul said it is *the kindness of God* that *leads you to repentance.* (Romans 2:4 NASB).

And King David said it this way: *He rewrites the text of my life when I open the book of my heart to His eyes...He makes my life complete when I place all the pieces before him...He stood me up on a wide-open field, and I stood there saved, surprised to be loved.* (Psalm 18 MSG, verses 24, 20, and 19, in that order)

What are the messy parts of your story?

Are you cringing as you think about it? Start there.

Ask God to show you how to open your heart to His eyes.

Let him love you in the mess, tend to the shame, and lead you into something or someone new.

After all, *We love because He first loved us.* (1 John 4:19)

> *Michelle Van Vliet is a pastor's wife, writer, and speaker residing in Turlock, California. As a graduate of the Renovaré Institute of Christian Spiritual Formation, her honest and energetic approach offers a fresh perspective of discipleship that moves beyond living for Jesus to envisioning a life of joyful companionship with Him.*

DIFFERENT KINDS OF LOVE

Sydney Smalling

Kristen paced the floor in her bedroom. In her arms, the sixteen-year-old held the brown aviator jacket that her best friend, Evelyn Thames, had lent to her.

Just a few hours before, Evelyn had been driving home from school when another car crashed into hers. An ambulance was called and rushed her to the hospital.

The hospital was keeping her overnight. Kristen prayed that everything would be okay. She'd tried to visit but Evelyn had been asleep.

At school the next day, everything was normal. Except for the fact that her friend wasn't there. Not many other people had heard about the accident.

She wore Evelyn's jacket walking home along her normal route. She had earphones on, listening to her favorite songs.

As she walked, she noticed a dark-haired boy around her age standing next to the chain link fence. Curious, Kristen walked over to see what was going on.

On the other side of the fence, a small, white, fluffy kitten crouched next to a bush.

The boy turned and noticed her. He had been trying to lure the kitten to the other side of the fence.

"Help me get him over here. His back leg looks like it's injured."

Kristin looked down at the small tomcat. He must've been only a few weeks old, because his eyes hadn't changed colors yet. His fur was mostly white, with a few dark points. He was adorable.

She quickly reached into her backpack and pulled out her sandwich. "I have this."

"Perfect!"

After a few minutes of coaxing, the kitten slowly approached them. The boy pulled the fence up enough for him to slip under.

Kristin scooped the small cat into her arms.

He meowed. She set him on the sidewalk, but he stayed at her feet and meowed again. He was still hungry.

"What's your name?" the boy asked.

"Kristen." She petted the cat's soft fur.

"I'm Luke. Thanks for helping me...and the kitten." He laughed.

Kristen smiled. "No problem. It's nice to meet you."

"You can keep him if you want to," Luke added.

She nodded hesitantly. The kitten meowed.

They parted ways, and Kristen went home with the kitten, saying a quick prayer that Mom would let her keep him.

She set him on the couch and begged her mom. Luckily, her mom said yes.

The next day, she went to visit Evelyn in the hospital. Kristin was happy to learn her friend only suffered a broken leg. She told Evelyn about how she rescued a kitten—and about Luke.

Evelyn laughed at the part about meeting the boy. "Can I come visit your kitten?"

Kristin grinned. "Of course. Try and come see him tomorrow."

Evelyn smiled.

"I'm glad I rescued him, he's so much fun."

"And of course, you can't forget about Luke!" her friend teased.

Kristin laughed. She suddenly remembered her friend's jacket, and held it out to her. Evelyn shook her head. "You can keep it. You'll probably use it more than me."

"Are you sure?"

"Of course! That's what friends do, right?"

Evelyn joked. "It sounds like you love this kitten more than me!"

They both laughed.

Kristin smiled. "Well, I do love the kitten. But the love I have for you is different—you're my best friend." And, she thought to herself, maybe someday she could love Luke too.

Sydney Smalling is a middle school student in California. She loves to read, write, and play with her three cats. Her favorite authors are Kendare Blake and Suzanne Collins. Sydney is so happy that her story was published last year, and hopes to keep writing in the future.

AN OUTPOURING OF LOVE

Lisa Braxton

Alex squeezed my hand as we left the doctor's office. "I'm sorry this is happening to you," he said.

A week before, a radiology technician sat at a table behind my head. I watched the monitor, straining my neck to see the screen. An image of my left kidney appeared. It looked like a bright, bean-shaped silhouette. On the other side of the screen, I saw what appeared as a smudge. I turned my head so I didn't have to keep looking at it.

"You're trembling. Do you need another blanket?" the technician asked.

"What is the smudge I see on the screen there? What does it mean?"

"Your doctor will give you the results when you see him," she said.

"How long will the dye from the IV stay in my system?" I asked.

"It will be gone by the time you see your doctor at the end of the week," she said.

☙

As I prepared to retire for the evening, I knelt at the foot of the bed.

"Dear Lord, You see the damage in my right kidney. Please bring it back to life. Lead me to some medicine and make it normal again." I crawled into bed working hard to breathe. My lungs felt shrunken with the air squeezed out of them. "Breathe for me, Lord," I whispered, trying to fall asleep.

My thoughts raced back several months. Alex, an intelligent man of God I had met at church, had asked me to marry him. We'd spent time discussing anything and everything at length and growing to know and love each other. We had planned the wedding of my dreams at a Colonial Revival style mansion with beautiful gardens. I looked forward to a new and exciting chapter in my life.

With all these plans ahead of me, I refused to believe anything would alter my dream. I thought the renal scan would confirm an error in the initial lab test results. Still, I slept fitfully.

Now, days later, after the renal scan, Alex and I sat in the urologist's office.

"I'm sorry, Lisa, your right kidney has a blockage. There's not much function at all," the doctor said. "But on the bright side, your left kidney is working as it should. Many people go through a lifetime with only one kidney. Would you like to see a nephrologist, a kidney specialist, to try to determine the reason for the blockage?" the doctor asked.

"Yes, why not. I don't think it will hurt. Let's see what we can find out," I said.

Alex walked me to my car. "Would it be okay if I hugged you?" he asked.

He wrapped his arms around me, but all I could think about were the words the doctor had said, *Many people go through a lifetime with only one kidney*. We got into our separate cars and drove away.

My doctor's words repeated in the back of my mind in the weeks leading up to the appointment with the kidney doctor. I tried to keep myself busy working on a seating chart for my wedding reception. I sifted through CDs of music to find the song I wanted played when my father walked me down the aisle of the mansion's ballroom.

Days later, Alex and I walked hand-in-hand into the kidney doctor's office.

"Make sure you write down all the doctor says so we can talk about it later," Alex said always thinking through details. "We don't want to forget any of it."

The doctor entered the room. "We're going to need to run more tests," he said. "There may be a problem with your other kidney."

Numbness crept through my mind. I didn't want to hear or believe his words. I rang my hands in my lap. In a moment, I realized all of my hopes rested in the remaining kidney. If my right kidney had damage what quality of life would I have? What kind of partner would I be to Alex?

"Will I have to go on dialysis?" I asked.

"The tests should tell us what's going on. Let's not get ahead of ourselves," the doctor said.

I already had.

As Alex and I walked out of the office, my thoughts drifted back.

For years, no one came along who seemed right for me. I accepted what I thought was God's plan. Then, in my late 40s, I met Alex.

Early in our relationship, I had to tell him about damage done internally due to previous surgeries. The surgery took away all hope I had of ever having a child.

Is it possible the stents put in place to help me heal from the surgeries, ended up causing more damage? Could it have led to the blockage in my kidney? The thoughts continued to plague me.

After hearing what the nephrologist had to say that day, I didn't feel comfortable involving Alex any further with my problems. He had a teenage daughter who would soon start college. He didn't need to be burdened with a disabled wife who would have mounting medical bills. I thought I should let him out of the engagement. I prayed, asking God if I was making the right decision.

Unable to sleep, I sent an email to my pastor asking him to pray to help me cope with my medical problems and the decision I felt I had to make about Alex.

The following Sunday as I sat in the pew reading the church bulletin before service began, I was surprised to hear my name called. The pastor asked me to come to the altar. The ministerial staff, in their vestments and clergy robes, came down from the pulpit and surrounded me. The congregation joined in prayer. After the church service, the pastor emeritus, who'd had his own recent medical struggles, pulled me aside, gave me a hug, and said he would be praying for me.

The intense prayer and outpouring of love I received gave me the strength to face my upcoming appointment with the nephrologist. I also knew I had to have the conversation with Alex.

After church, I went straight to his place.

"Alex, you don't have to marry me. It's not fair to you to go through this or have to deal with the medical bills. I'll be okay if you—"

"Leaving you never even crossed my mind," he said.

ༀ

With Alex at my side during the next appointment, the doctor gave me the results of the additional tests.

"What I see in your blood work should not be harmful in the long term. Your good kidney is functioning fine. You will need to watch it closely. I want you to come back periodically to have your kidney monitored."

I turned and smiled at Alex. I wanted to run out of the office as soon as possible before the doctor changed his mind.

Alex and I walked out of the doctor's office relieved at the news. I looked up at him and couldn't help but smile again. This was the man who made a commitment to me the day he put a ring on my finger, but showed me the depth of his love and commitment when I needed it most.

Lisa Braxton is a former newspaper and television journalist. Her stories have been published in **Vermont Literary Review**, **Women of Color Anthology**, **Inspire Joy**, *and* **Chicken Soup for the Soul**. *She received honorable mention for this essay in the Writer's Digest 84th annual writing contest. Her website is* www.lisabraxton.com.

LOVE LOOKS LIKE JOY

Rachel Dodge

My freshman year of college was by far the loneliest time of my life. I was far from my small-town friends and family, in the middle of a giant new city, and the relentless ache of homesickness was like a fist twisting in my gut. I wondered if anyone else felt the way I did—like the wind had been permanently knocked from my chest.

In the dorms, I lived in a cramped room with a girl I'd never met. Outside my door was a long hall of seventeen other rooms. Chaos and noise surrounded me. Radios blared, girls laughed and shrieked, doors slammed, and sirens screamed outside my window. There was no quiet place, no stillness there.

And part of me was glad. The constant activity and commotion helped beat back the waves of loneliness that threatened to overwhelm and drown me as I went to bed each night.

On Saturday nights, everyone was out looking for a party. I hadn't gone to any parties in high school, but since the alternative was staying in my room alone, I went out. There were people everywhere, walking the streets, yelling and laughing, going from party to party. Huge crowds spilled out into the yards of the fraternity houses and music pounded against the masses of dancing bodies. The energy and excitement was electrifying.

But while Saturday evenings were an exhilarating whirlwind of sound and fury, Sunday mornings were silent and still. No one got up before noon. No one wanted to go to breakfast. And *no one* wanted to go to church.

I had grown up going to church, so in college I still got up every Sunday and walked to the campus church alone. I was the only student who attended. Sometimes the girls on my floor would say they wanted to come with me, but every Sunday morning when I knocked on their doors, they either didn't answer or declined with an excuse. It got really old, really fast. I longed for comfort and community.

Midway through the fall semester, I had met a lot of people and was extremely busy and active on campus, but my heart still ached. I missed my family, my home, my friends, and my church. I liked the girls in my dorm, but they were all a big mess just like me. There didn't seem to be anyone to turn to; everyone was just as lost and miserable as I was.

And then I met Joy. She was a soft-spoken, blue-eyed senior, who lived at the other end of the dorm floor from me. I didn't know why any senior would want to live in the freshman dorms, but she was kind, comforting, and safe.

My first real memory of her was when I was trying to find a ride to the train station one weekend so I could go home for my birthday. I had asked everyone I could think of who owned a car and hadn't found anyone to take me. When I mentioned my problem to Joy, she immediately said, "I'll drive you." I almost cried with relief.

And from then on, whenever I needed anything, Joy was there for me. If I needed a ride, day or night, she drove me. If I needed to talk, she listened. She stayed up late to get to know me, took an interest in me, and shared her life with me. When I ran to her door at 5:45 a.m. one morning, after missing the van from campus to my rowing team practice, she squinted at me in the bright light of the hallway, disappeared for a moment, and then handed me her keys and told me where to find her car.

One day, Joy asked me if I'd like to come with her to the Christian fellowship group she attended on campus. I was curious but said no when I heard that her group was of a different denomination than the one I'd grown up with. For me, that was a deal breaker.

But Joy didn't give up. She kept loving me. She was consistent and always there.

And she kept inviting me. She didn't badger me, but every so often she would invite me to church or to her Bible study. She even took some of us to a Christian concert one night. It wasn't until the end of the year that I finally tried out her campus fellowship group. I liked the people, but I didn't like the way the Bible contradicted my liberal views. I went and listened but kept my distance.

At the end of the year, Joy graduated, got a job, got engaged, and moved off campus, but she was there for me more than ever my sophomore year. She drove to campus every Sunday to take me to church and back again, even though it was far out of her way. She invited me to gatherings at her apartment, gave me a key so I could study there when she was at work, and made me part of her life. She sent me cards in the mail with little notes of encouragement and Scripture verses. When we spent time together, I would ask question after question about the Bible and about what Jesus did on the cross. I started attending the campus fellowship group regularly and joined a small group Bible study.

I had always believed in Jesus, but one question began to echo through my mind that year: "What do they have that I don't have?" I saw that Joy and her friends absolutely loved Jesus, enjoyed the Bible, and had a deep relationship with God. I wanted what they had.

At one point, my Bible study leader asked me, "Have you ever asked Jesus to be your personal Savior?" I was offended at first, but as I began to think about it, I knew deep in my heart that I never had. I had been a "Christian" all my life. How in the world could I admit that I had never been saved? But one spring night, as I laid on the floor of my dark apartment bedroom, finally at the end of myself, I did just that. I cried out to Jesus and asked Him to come into my heart and take over my entire life forever. I'll never forget the image I saw in my mind's eye of Jesus above me on the ceiling, arms open wide, inviting me into His arms.

From that point on, I began to grow in the grace and knowledge of the Lord Jesus Christ. I started to pray and read my Bible each night before bed. I didn't change immediately, but I began to steadily change in every area of my life. And Joy was always there.

Joy was the definition of a faithful friend. She loved me through many seasons and countless questions, breakups, and heartaches. She was an anchor for me when I felt like everything was falling apart; she pulled me through when I thought I wouldn't make it. She was the embodiment of love.

What I didn't realize until much later was that during my senior year of high school, when Joy was getting ready for her senior year in college, Jesus had asked her a question: Would she be willing to leave behind the comfort of her life, her friends, and her apartment to go live in the freshman dorms "for such a time as this?" Her answer, which no doubt echoed through the courts of Heaven, was simple: "Send me, Lord!"

I thank Jesus for sending Joy to live on my dorm floor, out of all the freshman dorms on campus, so that I could know Him personally. Joy loved me like she did because she chose to live her life like Jesus. She had a boyfriend, a job, a community, and a church. She wasn't lonely or sad. She had a full life and plenty of friends. But like Jesus, Joy chose to leave her happy home in order to step into my mess.

I can only imagine all that Joy endured that year for the sake of the Gospel, but when she chose to leave the comfort zone of her life in order to enter the construction zone of mine, she made an eternal impact. I don't know if anyone else on my dorm floor became a Christian because of Joy's choice to live on mission that year; I just know that I became a Christian because of Joy. And to me, Love looks like Joy.

❧

"Therefore, I endure everything for the sake of the elect, that they also may obtain the salvation that is in Christ Jesus with eternal glory." (2 Timothy 2:10 ESV)

Rachel Dodge is an English instructor, writer, and speaker who loves to tell stories that bring God glory. She is first and foremost a wife, mother, and servant of Jesus. A passionate prayer warrior, Rachel enjoys encouraging and equipping others to grow closer to Jesus and understand God's Word.

ELLA'S HEART

E. V. Sparrow

A priest stood beneath tall, stained glass windows and raised his hands. Bells tinkled. His words droned, escorted by a trail of incense smoke wafted upward with his swing of the brass thurible, "Bless…keep you…His face shine upon you…peace."

Ella sat on the end of a row of pews forming a large half circle. Her hazel eyes narrowed and scanned the congregation, until her floral headscarf slipped across one eye. She adjusted it with the help of her husband, Jack.

Secret plans for Jack's future bloomed within her heart. *Cancer, I've beaten you for seven years…and I'm exhausted. You pull me toward death and cause pain to my loved ones. Well, you can't win…I won't let you destroy Jack!* Ella linked her arm through Jack's and lifted her chin. *My tender Jack must remarry.* Her gaze scrutinized Margaret across the aisle—a delicate, stylish, white-haired widow dressed in a red cape. *Her late husband, Tom, was a lot like Jack.* Ella nodded.

Soft worship lyrics accompanied by the harmony of blended instruments faded into silence.

☙

Ella's family joined the worship band members in the sanctuary for a discussion of lunch plans.

Janine, Ella's daughter, spoke above the babble. "Hey, it's Daryl's turn to decide again."

Jack reminded the group of an awful experience from his son-in-law's last choice of restaurant. "Those hamburgers were the texture of cardboard! I think we should give your turn to someone else."

"They were veggie burgers!"

Ella tugged on Janine's sleeve and drew her several steps away from the group.

Janine tucked her dark hair behind one ear and bent toward Ella.

Ella whispered, "I chose a lady."

Janine jerked upright. "What?" She held her breath and glanced up, then forced a smile. "Hi Dad, you're stealthy."

Ella turned and discovered Jack near her shoulder.

"What are you up to now, darlin'?" He winked at Ella and raised a brow. Jack's vivid blue eyes studied their faces.

"Never you mind." Ella shook her head.

☙

Janine looked away. Tears choked her. *This can't be happening.* Her dark gaze landed on the stage with the band's instruments and music stands. "I'll clear the stage." *God, why don't you heal Mom? You can do it...don't take her.* Janine reached for her music stand, and knocked it with her knuckles. It tipped backward. She grabbed for the flying sheet music, but her shaky hands missed.

The papers fluttered to the floor. Janine stared for a moment. *Why does Mom insist on Dad remarrying?* She bent down and reached for the stand. *What do I say?* Janine rose and bumped the guitar. It slid sideways. "Stop!" She dropped the stand to rescue the guitar from a crash. A hollow *twang* reverberated from the stage. "Good heavens."

The group chatter dwindled away.

Janine stamped her foot, and wiped away tears.

Daryl called out, "Wait, I'll help you!"

"I'm good!" Janine waved above her head. She gathered the sheet music from the floor, her back to the group. A tear splashed onto the papers.

Daryl touched Janine's elbow. "Are you in a hurry?"

"A little bit."

He squeezed her shoulders. "Okay, love."

Janine pointed at the instruments. "Please, ask Dad to help you load up." She stacked the papers with her face averted.

"Are you worried about Mom? She looks pretty tired today."

"Yes." Janine opened her case and slipped in the music sheets. "I'll fetch Mom and we'll meet you outside in a few minutes."

"Sure, love." Daryl turned toward the group and clapped his hands. "Hey everyone, let's load up and you, too, Dad!"

Janine found Ella in conversation with a woman in the crowded lobby. "Mom…"

Ella swung around.

Janine leaned against the wall with folded arms, and glared.

Ella smiled at the woman. "Let's talk tomorrow." She followed Janine into the sanctuary.

"Mom, who did you choose?"

☙

Ella tipped her head in the direction of the lobby. "It's Margaret. Remember her late husband, Tom? He sang in the choir with your dad."

"Yes."

"Well, Margaret and I…" Ella swayed. Her unsteady hand grasped a pew near her, and she scooted in. "Come sit with me…a moment."

Janine settled next to her.

"We became acquainted when we exchanged used altar linens for clean ones at each other's homes." Ella twisted her loose wedding rings around her finger. "Sometimes, the four of us went out. I chose Margaret because your dad is comfortable with her."

Janine clenched her teeth. "Mom, you're trying to control everything. How can you choose a wife for him?"

"He won't do well alone." Ella laid her thin arm across her daughter's shoulders. "Dear, this is important to me—"

"I'm so upset with you! This is wrong." Janine shook her head. "Dad's still your husband!" She softly sobbed.

Ella hugged Janine. "We've been together for fifty-six years. I love him and I'm not leaving him by choice."

"You need to fight and get well!"

"I'm exhausted from the battle, so I'm making my peace—"

"Mom…" Janine searched for a tissue in her purse. "I still don't understand."

"I don't expect you to understand. This is between me and God."

Jack and Daryl peered around the exit doors. Daryl waved them forward, "Hey, loves, we're ready to go. Our stomachs are growling."

Janine sniffed into the tissue and cleared her throat. She leaned over and kissed Ella's cheek. "Did you rest long enough?"

Ella nodded, and rose with Janine's help. "Another thing…I read about grief. People need some time…but your dad tends to get depressed and lonely."

Janine huffed, "Mom, I really don't want you to worry, and I don't want to argue with you."

"Allow me this, Janine…please? I think the best strategy is to give Margaret rides to church. Then invite her for choir lunches, and bring her to family activities."

"I'll try, Mom…you know we'll take care of Dad, don't you?" She kissed her mother's cheek. "And we'll trust God with this, okay?"

"I'm just…worried." *God, what if Jack blames You? It breaks my heart—*

Janine grasped her arm and led her from the chill of the church into the warm sunshine.

Ella squinted when she emerged from the shadows into the bright light. Her steps halted, while she waited for her eyes to adjust.

Birds twittered among the pink-blossomed trees.

She looked up. Bright white clouds parted. Streaks of sunrays touched the earth. *Heaven…Lord, now I can rest, and think about home…with You.*

ℭ

Five years after Ella's passing, Jack courted Margaret in a measured process that Ella intuitively believed would work for him.

Their church family watched and rejoiced.

Jack and Margaret married and traveled the world on several cruises. They enjoyed new love and life together for twelve years, until Jack passed.

❦

E. V.'s published articles are "Meaghan O'Meara's Bowl" and "Don't Bypass Joy, My Love." Widely travelled, muralist turned author/ illustrator, E.V.'s published illustrations are in **Little Known Tales in California History***.*

My Unrelenting Love

Jean Johnson

My dear child, I intimately knew you before you were born.

I shaped your personality and infused it with My likeness.

I chose your parents and the part of the world where you would live.

Child, do you know that your spirit is intertwined with Mine?

You are My beautiful and divine masterpiece.

Just as you are, you are of great value to the Trinity,

(Father God, Jesus, and Holy Spirit)

You are worth more than any costly treasure here on earth.

My love is everlasting, intense, unrelenting, and jealous for you.

Will you come to Me and open your heart to receive My love for you?

My love is incomparable and nothing like earthly love, which can be distorted.

Come, dear child, will you let go of the lies that hinder receiving My love for you?

I invite you to draw your heart toward Me, and allow Me to fill you.

I, Jesus, the lover of your soul, will never stop pursuing you.

I have never forsaken you, nor left you alone. No never!

I long to hear your voice, as you search for Me.

Even now, I sing and dance over you, My precious child.

Jean Johnson's avid love of reading and writing throughout her life stemmed from those early childhood years when she read stories to her blind father. In May 2014, Jean graduated with English honors. Currently, she writes short stories, articles, book reviews for her grief group, devotionals, poems, and blogs.

PRAYER AND A BATCH OF COOKIES

by
Wendi Johnson
As told to Karen Foster

I pulled my baking sheet out of the oven and inhaled the sweet scent of chocolate chip cookies. They were too much to resist, but when I bit into a warm cookie, my tears came—again. These cookies were bound for the male inmates in one of our state prisons.

Would one of the three men who'd killed my husband be eating them? I hoped so. But I never would have believed that thought was possible.

On September 27, 2005, my twenty-year-old son, Brandon, had left a message at work for me to call him. I prepared the examining room for the next chiropractic patient, and sat at the reception desk to return his call. I presumed my son wanted to talk about a job interview he'd had that day. I was wrong. Without explanation, he said, "Auntie Dawn is coming to get you."

My heart froze. "Why is my sister picking me up?"

Brandon dodged my questions, but right before he hung up, he said, "Don't worry, Mom. I'll take care of you."

My stomach lurched. I thought of calling my husband, Kim, but my body started shaking. What if something had happened to him? I pressed my hand over my mouth and ran to the restroom. When my sister arrived, her eyes were red and puffy. "Where's Kim?" I grabbed her hand. "Is he dead?"

She nodded. The room swirled, and I collapsed into her arms with a gut-wrenching scream. How could my husband be dead? I'd talked with him on the phone during lunch. Didn't Kim say he'd left work early and was home? We'd joked and laughed. Was it a heart attack? What if the gun he'd been cleaning for the hunting season had accidentally gone off? His final words…"I love you, darling"…squeezed my heart.

I leaned against my sister and urged her, "Get me home!"

Yellow caution tape sealed off my street. I stretched my neck to see beyond the police cars with their flashing blue lights. "Where's my son?" I cried, pacing back and forth. "I want my son!"

Right then, Brandon ran up to me. Chests heaving, we clung to each other and wept. My son told me he'd come home and found Kim, his stepdad, lying on the basement floor in a pool of blood. He'd been beaten and shot in the head. Many of our electronics and guns were gone including the handgun used to kill my husband.

My mind reeled. Who would be so cruel?

Two days passed before the police allowed me to go into my home. I was numb as they escorted me through the house and questioned me. When I entered our master bedroom, I gasped. The blue-gray T-shirt Kim had worn the last time I'd seen him was splayed across our bed. I grabbed his T-shirt—the closest thing to hugging Kim—and breathed in my husband's clean scent. Tears flooding my eyes, I slumped like a rag doll on the bed and wept.

After Kim's funeral, I moved back into the house with my son. We installed a burglar alarm, but it didn't alleviate our fears. What if the murderer was someone we knew? I kept the alarm's panic button with me at all times.

Nights were the worst. My mind searched for answers. Listened for the slightest sound. Rushed to Brandon's bedside whenever nightmares woke him up and he needed me. My only comfort was prayer and Deuteronomy 31:6. "Be strong and courageous…for the Lord your God goes with you; he will never leave you nor forsake you."

A year after Kim's death, the handgun was found which led to the arrest of three men. However, relief morphed into impatience as I waited another year and a half for the trial. During that time, Kairos Prison Ministry came to our church. They were organizing an intensive weekend Bible study at one of our state prisons. They asked for volunteers to bake cookies for the prisoners.

I crossed my arms. I hadn't baked cookies since Kim's death and I wasn't going to bake them for some criminal. My back stiffened as I leaned against the cushioned pews. Preach the Gospel if you like, but I want justice.

I rushed out of church and drove home. Although the men were behind bars, I double bolted the door and threw my car keys on the granite kitchen counter. They landed with a clanking thud next to a package of store-bought cookies.

Bake cookies? Why not ask me to forgive Kim's murderers? I breathed deep and listened to Christian praise music to calm my nerves. Lord, it's going to take more than a batch of cookies to soften my heart.

And then I had to face my enemy. For seven days, in September 2008, I sat in the courtroom behind the two men who killed my husband and stared at the back of their heads. The third man had pled guilty and testified at the trial. As I listened to the prosecuting attorney, I learned the men needed money, had mistaken our house for someone else's, and thought the place was empty.

What if's replayed in my head. If only the seventeen-year-old man who pulled the trigger had stayed in school that day. If only they'd entered our neighbor's house, my husband would still be alive. If only Kim's pistol had been in the gun safe.

I'd never seen the crime scene photographs. Seeing the horror of Kim's final moments crushed my heart. I wept countless tears. My anger grew. I kept waiting for the men to face me. Beg for my forgiveness. Even when I was on the witness stand and excused myself because I became sick to my stomach, their cold, dark eyes stared straight ahead as though I were invisible.

The jury found them guilty of first-degree murder. They each received a life sentence. End of story, or so I thought. Negative thoughts consumed me. I tried to forget the past for the sake of my family and health. I even volunteered to bake cookies for Kairos Prison Ministry.

As I stirred in the chocolate chips into the dough, tears rolled down my cheeks. What would Kim say if he saw me baking cookies for convicted felons? I wiped my eyes and set the oven timer. Lord, remove the hate and make my spirit as sweet as these cookies. Use them for your glory.

As the scent of chocolate chip cookies filled the kitchen, I prayed for the men who killed my husband. They weren't evil men. The poor decisions they'd made in life became a domino effect that led to Kim's death. Now, they suffered the consequences. Where was their hope? Did they know about God's love and grace? Should I write them and share the Gospel?

Another year passed and I kept baking cookies for prisoners, but my heart wouldn't rest until I wrote the three men who killed Kim. "God loves you, regardless of what you've done," I said. "I've forgiven you, and God's willing to forgive you if you turn to Him."

The following month, I gasped when I opened my mailbox and saw the envelope's return address. My hands shook as I read the prisoner's neat, handwritten letter. "I'm sorry for all the pain I caused you and your family. Thank you, Wendi, for your letter. I prayed for a sign that I'd been forgiven."

I clutched the letter to my chest. How long had I waited for an apology? As if—I'm sorry—could ease the pain. When all along, this man had been praying and waiting too. The young man who pulled the trigger also replied with heartfelt words that made me weep. God had been working in all our lives to heal, redeem, restore.

When another organization, Forsyth Prison Ministry, asked for volunteers to participate in their Sunday services at Cherry State Prison, my hand went up. On a summer evening in 2014, I walked through the metal detector of that prison with a plate of cookies and a heart filled with praise. The next year, they asked me to share my story.

My knees wobbled as I stepped in front of a hundred inmates dressed in grey T-shirts and green pants. Their eyes widened as I described Kim's gruesome death. I told them I'd forgiven the men who murdered him and continued to write to them. Some inmates wiped their eyes. Others shook their heads.

"For all have sinned and fallen short of God's glory," I said, quoting Romans 3:23. "No one is beyond God's love and grace."

People ask how I could forgive the men who killed my husband. Sometimes, I ask myself that question when I see Kim's shirt tucked in my dresser drawer. Or when I bake chocolate chip cookies for prison ministry. I tell them God's love softened my heart, one batch of cookies at a time.

Karen Foster is a freelance writer, blogger, and speaker. Her devotions and true first-person stories have appeared in multiple magazines, ezines, and four other Inspire anthologies. Karen especially loves being a ghostwriter and giving voice to other people's stories. Visit her website at KarenFosterMinistry.com.

Previously printed in Bible Advocate's ezine: Now What? 2016

TRUSTING GOD AND GROWING IN LOVE

Dr. W. Alan Dixon, Sr.

For some people loving others comes easy. For me, showing love toward those in my life at work and home is difficult. Over time, I am learning how to better show love to colleagues and those close to me personally. God is using my experiences to help me overcome my love deficiency.

Organizational leaders have taught American workers to focus on task completion and to use logic to solve work-related issues. Start with the end in mind, or review past similar scenarios to discover acceptable outcomes. Make sure your process is methodical, not emotional. At no point, can we even think about saying the word love in the office without potential detrimental circumstances, or calls from Human Resources. Leaders frown upon workers using feelings to problem solve in many workplaces, even if normal reasoning does not lead to success. Regardless of the frustration, pain, or suffering we experience, employers teach us to suck it up and deal with the situation emotionless.

As Christians, Jesus actually commands us to love one another as He loved us (John 15:12). Yet that is in direct opposition to what our bosses tell us. So, what is right? How can we follow Christ and our organizational leaders without compromising our principles? In the secular environment, kindness can be misconstrued, so it is vital to take precautions. For example, while we can offer kind words or do kind actions, we can choose not being alone with the opposite sex and not allowing inappropriate touching. The limitations are actually protective, and help us prevent violating work boundaries. What love language do I use for success in the world that also helps me learn to love people as Jesus loves me?

As a new leader, and new Christian, I struggled. I did not know how to help, or what to say, when I saw my coworkers and colleagues stressed. Even worse, I am not the most expressive person, so showing love is simply unnatural to me, not only in work situations, but also in my own personal relationships. I cannot speak for all men, yet I know many men I have worked with, both Christian and non-believers, that have expressed the same difficulty in expressing love.

Christ showed us love. He based all of His actions in love. His examples demonstrated how to love others. So why do I continue struggle so much? Scripture revealed the first lesson to help me better understand God's plan. *Trust in the LORD with all your heart; do not depend on your own understanding. Seek his will in all you do. And he will show you which path to take* (Proverbs 3:5-6 NLT). Unfortunately, I compile my unnatural ability to love with skepticism. "Yeah, Lord, that is easy to do. Trust You, and miraculously all my decisions become clear and loving others is now easy? So far, that plan has not worked well for me."

What I fail to understand is God did not say how His plans would all work out. He did not provide me with a formula for success, or a logical roadmap. Like my issues at work, I attempt to use logic to improve my understanding, but God just asks that we trust Him. Where I struggle in my relationships, I began to realize I have the same struggle with God. Trusting him with ALL of my heart. Such a little word, yet it has amazing meaning. Perhaps God is softening my heart, all of my heart, through Scriptures, so I can better do what He has planned.

Psalm 33:13-15 (NLT) summates it very well: *The LORD looks down from heaven and sees the whole human race. From his throne he observes all who live on earth. He made their hearts, so he understands everything they do.* God already knows my woes and difficulties. He knows how much I have been hurt and how I guard my heart as a result. He knows every thought before I do, and at times, I still fail to trust Him. I am learning trust and love go hand in hand. I have to trust God first, and He will show me how to love others the way Jesus loved us. I am on an ongoing journey to learn how to love. Thus far, I have filled this difficult excursion to better love others with self-created roadblocks.

At work, care comes from taking time to listen to people when they need to talk, remembering to ask about important events, or sharing kind or encouraging words. Small acts of generosity, like buying donuts for the office, can show love to those at work. We can show real concern by helping younger workers not make the same mistakes we did, or simply by being authentic. Christ, who lives in our heart, can help us if we allow Him to direct our paths in the workspace.

Learning to love at home remains even more challenging. Even though my wife of nearly twenty-five years is my most intimate partner, the struggle to show her love is real. Being her caregiver over the last five years has softened my heart, but not melted it. I try to use kinder words and not be frustrated when she cannot do something for herself, but I am still a work in progress. I know God is working to make me more like Him, despite my human resistance to change. It does seem like it is worth it as Scripture continues to mold me into something I am not used to being, someone who is learning to love others. I know me, and I know it's God not me making these dramatic changes.

I hope and pray that, over time, God will continue to nudge me through His infallible Word and help me to trust more and to love more, but it is an ongoing challenge for me. My goal is simple. By the time I go to meet Jesus face-to-face, I want to be able to say I lived by the new commandment He gave us in John 13:34-35 (NLT). *So now I am giving you a new commandment: Love each other. Just as I have loved you, you should love each other. Your love for one another will prove to the world that you are my disciples.* In the meantime, I will keep on my mission, stay in God's Word daily, trust in Him, and love His people a little more each day.

Dr. W. Alan Dixon, Sr. resides in Northern California with his best friend and wife Xochitl. He has two adult sons, AJ and Xavier, a daughter-in-law, Mallory, and a doggy daughter, Jazzy. He writes articles and devotions to encourage and build up new leaders, who will in turn build the future.

LOVE CONQUERS FEAR

Barbara Stocker

Moisture built in my eyes. Heat rushed across my face. Could the doctor see my heart beating through my top? He wore a mask, gloves, and sterile gown. Though I tried to concentrate on the words he said, my mind stuck on one word. Tuberculosis.

And, suddenly, thoughts hurled me back to an earlier time.

❧

Widowed with seven children, my mother spent her days working hard to provide. By six months old, I faced a life-threatening illness. She took me to the hospital, thinking I would not survive. She could not afford the critical care the doctor said I would need due to the tuberculosis that had invaded my small system. Out of love for her baby she couldn't care for, she surrendered me, as a ward of the court, to the hospital with the hopes that I would survive.

For the next five years, I lived in a metal-barred crib, often tied down while in an oxygen tent. The venetian-blind-covered window looked like bars to me. The blue sky, seen only through slits, remained just beyond my reach. I often heard voices in the hallway outside the room, as light drifted under the closed door.

The sanatorium remained the only home I knew. The nurses and doctors—my family. I called them half-faces though, because they always hid behind masks. Always seen. Never touched by love.

⁌⁍

As the masked doctor faced me, memories threatened to slam the door, trapping me once again.

"We believe you have tuberculosis again," he said. He handed me a mask and said, "The nurse will be here soon to take you to your isolation room."

As he left, suddenly, I struggled to get air. My mind raced toward my unborn baby and worry over whether I'd exposed my husband and my three-year-old child at home. I felt the door of my heart begin to close. Creaking. Looming with a feared impending conclusion.

The nurse came in pushing a wheelchair. My mind felt like a fog settled over it in confusion. I struggled to swallow threatening tears. We moved down the hall to the door with isolation tape across it. Next to the door sat a table with masks, hospital gowns, and gloves on top. *I want to go home. I want to see Michael. I want to have his arms around me whispering how much he loves me and telling me all would be okay.*

The door closed and I got into the gown. Picking up the phone next to the bed, with trembling fingers, I dialed my husband's work number. He answered on the first ring.

"Michael, I'm still at the hospital," I gulped fighting tears. "They think I have T.B. again. I'm in isolation. Oh, Michael—" the sobs broke through the words.

"I'll be right there. I love you. I'm on my way," he said before I could say anything else.

Crawling into the bed with its stark white sheets, I wiped tears off my cheeks with the hospital pillowcase. The muscles in my face tightened. My back went rigid. Tingles ran down my arms and I ran my hands up and down them. I pulled my legs up against my chest and wrapped my arms around them. No words came when I tried to pray. I gasped for air through the moans.

A creak sounded behind me. I wiped my face again and looked toward where the noise had come from. Michael walked to the bed and pushed down the bedrail. He slowly sat down, turned, stretched out behind me, and wrapped his arms around me. His grip tightened with each gasp of tears.

"I'm here honey. You're going to be okay," he whispered against my head.

I turned my face as far as possible toward him.

"You're supposed to wear a mask, gloves, and gown," I said.

"I just saw you this morning," he said and shrugged his broad shoulders.

"I needed to see your face," I said.

His eyes watered and the corners of his mouth turned up slightly.

I took a deep breath. The room had not changed. The smell of alcohol still permeated the space. But, a shudder escaped my lips and my breathing returned to normal. We were together.

Turning over to face him, I rested my head against his shoulder.

Michael began to pray while he rubbed his hand up and down my back.

"Lord, we need Your help. Please heal Barbara's lungs. Give her a calmness and peace. Help us to trust You through this. Please help our unborn baby to be okay. Help our little Christine at home not to get sick. We pray for You to help Barbara come home soon. We love You, Father. We're going to put our trust in You."

Michael lowered his lips to mine for only a moment. He stood up from the bed, winked at me and said, "I love you. I'll be back soon."

Tests, x-rays, and doctor's examinations filled the next six days. Finally, the doctor said the best words I could have heard.

"It's not tuberculosis. You have double pneumonia. The dark shadows on your lungs are scars from the T.B. you had as a child."

I took a big breath and released it quickly. Once again, tears rolled down my cheeks. I didn't bother wiping them away.

"Thank You, Jesus," I whispered.

⁓

As I think back over these memories, I see God's faithfulness to love me even through my worst fear. When the doctor said, "T.B.," I thought lonely isolation once again loomed before me. The difference is, as a child, I didn't know God's love or the amazing love of a husband. God's love and faithfulness, hand in hand with Michael's, helped me walk through what could have ended much worse. No matter what, God would have brought us through, but we are thankful His love chose this wonderful outcome.

🦗

Barbara is a woman who has had a difficult journey but the Lord has restored her soul and given her beauty for ashes.

My Darling Daughter, A Love Letter from the Father

Terese Belme

My darling daughter, I have known you since before time began. I knew you the moment you were conceived in your mother's womb. I watched with delight as each part of you began to form. I shouted continually, "This is my girl. This is my princess!" That wonderful day finally arrived, the day you were born. I marked that date for all eternity because, you my princess, mean more to me than you will ever know.

I shouted to the world, "Come, look at My daughter, look at her beauty. Look at her tiny hands and her tiny feet." Oh, the plans I have for your life. Plans of hope, peace, and joy. Yes, even during the challenging times in life, you can have all these things.

I have watched you grow from an infant to a toddler. I was there when you took your first step, said your first word and your first tooth came in.

I was there when you were a child, and those older kids made fun of you and called you names. My heart hurt more than yours, and my love for you never faltered.

I was there when you put on your first pair of glasses, and when you needed braces for your teeth. I chaperoned your first dance and looked out for you, My darling daughter.

I went with you to high school and attended all your extracurricular events. No one was prouder of you than I when you scored your first basket, hit your first softball, swam your first lap, and gave *the* best speech ever! I was with you on those lonely nights when your friends were at a dance or hanging out at a friend's house, and you couldn't be with them. I have always promised to never leave you.

I long for you to know that you are accepted. You can come to Me, and I will accept you always. I am gentle and will give you rest for you soul.

I long for you to know how I adore you. Whenever I fix my gaze upon you, the radiance of your beauty shines from the inside out like the shimmering of precious gems when sunlight hits them. There is a strong family resemblance, and you will always be the apple of My eye.

I long for you to know that you are My beloved. My darling daughter, there isn't anything you could ever do to cause Me to stop loving you.

I long for you to know that you are blameless. It is true you live in a distorted and twisted generation, but you shine among this generation like a star in the sky.

I long for you to know how truly blessed you are. Indeed, blessed are you among women, simply because you are My daughter, and My love for you is a perpetual circle—it is never ending.

I long for you to know you are chosen. I have known all that you are since before time began and I chose you. You, my daughter, bring Me glory.

I long for you to know you are holy because I, your loving Father, am holy.

I long for you to know you are worthy. You have grown into a woman of noble character. You are worth far more than rubies. You are priceless to Me. In all you do, you work with eager hands. I see you are up early and retire late all for the sake of your family. I see.

My beautiful daughter, don't you know? You are like a beautiful garden, and I sing over you always. I nourish you day and night and watch over you non-stop.

You are Mine and I am yours and I love you. My darling daughter.

Terese is a continual student of God's amazing grace. Her heart and passion is to come alongside and teach others about their identity, authority, and inheritance in Jesus Christ as ambassadors to the kingdom of God. Terese resides with her husband and two of her three kids in Northern California.

Prince Charming Times Two

Beth Miller Cantrell

As a child, I talked of things I wanted in my husband. I thought what it would be like to love and marry Prince Charming, and how we'd live happily ever after. When I grew up, the fairytale prince and princess were tucked away. The happily ever after became hidden by the business of life. I let go of some childish fantasies when I met and married Charles. He was down to earth, romantic, and set my heart aflame.

We walked down the aisle a year later. He became my Prince Charming for over fifty years of marriage before he graduated to glory. I adjusted to surviving life alone, but had dreams of my Prince, who became only a memory in my heart.

There are clear recollections of the walks on the beach and hearing the wave's crash on the shore. Sitting on the sand dunes holding hands, and staying until the last ray of the fireball sun disappeared into the Pacific. His memory is in the golden warmth we shared in those God-given years watching the sunset. In the magnificent suspension of time, he held me and sang into my ear, "Let Me Call You Sweetheart."

Before he went to Heaven, Charles seriously said, "If I go home first, I don't want you to be lonely. Find another Prince Charming to love, and be a companion to him."

The single men in our small church were amazing but nowhere near my age, they were closer to the age of my son.

I considered and then tried Christian Mingle. Over the next months, I met three different men for lunch. It seemed like a futile search, and I was ready to give-up. The men were the right age, distinctive, and thoughtful. I hoped I wasn't stuck in childish thoughts, but none of them were keepers for me.

❧

Down the freeway in Vacaville, Allen's daughter encouraged him to try Christian dating. Allen's wife of fifty-eight years was in Heaven. On-line we made arrangements to meet. As I got out of my car in front of the Woodland Restaurant, Allen casually leaned against the front door railing.

The closer I approached, the more green-blue his eyes shone, matching the blue of his shirt. His cowboy boots and slightly bowed legs made me think of a Texan.

Did I still have a fantasy of a tall, dark, and handsome Prince Charming?

Allen's average height looked tall enough, as did his fair skin and red hair mingled with gray. He had the striking swagger of a cowboy. Not my childhood picture, but his first impression was appealing. As we exchanged greetings, I focused on his compelling smile. The awkwardness of a first meeting soon dissolved as he reached for my hand to climb the ramp, and open the door. Soon we were seated across a table from one another.

"How do you like Woodland?"

I lifted my head from the menu. His dancing eyes caught my breath with a slow intake of air. "This is my first time here. I like all the trees, and I'm curious about the Gibson Mansion, The Opera House, and the Agriculture Museum I saw online."

"That's good, for Woodland is one of my favorite small towns." He winked at me.

With a shiver, I melted.

"Maybe after we eat, we can take a short tour of downtown."

"That would be great. I'd like to know more. The town seems quaint and welcoming."

My chicken salad tasted fresh, but I was sorry I'd ordered a meal that took so much cutting and chewing. It was hard to carry on a conversation with a mouth full of lettuce. I was glad Allen ate slowly, enjoying his sizzling platter.

We lingered over the meal taking in the newness of each other.

When we stood to leave, I said, "I'd like to do the driving down Main Street."

"That will be fine. I'll navigate and tell you about the highlights."

We drove past Ludy's restaurant which was decorated with brightly colored banners. Allen said, "We will have to go there to eat sometime and check it out."

My mind raced and my heart pounded. *Wow! Does that mean we will have a second date? I hope so. This is the first man I've been attracted to since becoming a widow.*

We turned around and headed back down the blocks of Main Street. Allen got out and came around the car to shake my hand, giving me his now familiar smile. It's the kind of smile that you can't help but smile back. The warmth of his good-bye, made me want to stay longer.

As I drove east and he went west, I hoped our relationship would bloom. I reflected on the promising sign when he asked to see me again.

All the way home I had to pay attention to the traffic and not day-dream about Allen.

For three months, we talked on the phone most every night— about things of the Lord, about things we liked, about our feelings, and events from our pasts. We met every Wednesday at noon for lunch, at the sentimental place where we first met. After we tried many things on the lunch menu, we branched out. It wasn't about the food, but about becoming friends.

Ludy's dining area invited us in with long tables and some cozy booths. Entering through the vestibule we peered up into the high walls and ceiling covered with cowboy memorabilia. I delighted at Allen's shining eyes. He was at home with the cowboy theme. The building had a BBQ out on the back patio where the aroma of ribs and hamburgers floated up from the smoking grills. The restaurant's ambiance captured the southwest scenery of Allen's childhood, where he rode bareback in the wide-open fields of Texas.

Seated across the table, Allen kissed the back of my hand. My heart pranced, and I smiled back at him. Our many splendid moments mounted in my heart. From what Allen said, I knew he too was treasuring our times together. Our love for Jesus spilled over to our growing love for each other. The food had just enough spices to awaken our pallets without burning our mouths. As I drove home I thought about my new zest for life in my flaming heart.

Six months later, Allen drove around to a residential part of Woodland and found Reiff's Gas Station Museum. We held hands walking around the extra-long garage full of dozens of vintage gas pumps. Allen enjoyed seeing the side handles. It brought back memories of his pumping the lever to ten gallons as he forced gas up into an oblong glass measuring bowl, to then dispense into cars. His eyes sparkled when he recalled his teen years as a gas hop, and a gallon sold for ten cents.

As we parted for our homes, Allen pulled me into a hug and said, "Will you marry me?"

With a leap of my heart, I whispered, "Yes," and snuggled closer into his kiss.

Pondering life with Allen became all encompassing. After talks with my daughter and her husband and Allen's son and his wife, we considered our future. Our Christian walk was at the top of our lists. The growing love and companionship we shared came second. Third, we both were family oriented. Was there an illusion that we were too old and fooling ourselves in our joy? Were we too blinded by our love to become a geriatric prince and princess?

We were old yet we were ready to reach for that second chance at love.

Allen said, "Well, we have a total of one-hundred-eight years of marriage between us. With Jesus as our guide, we know how to be married and share the give and take of living."

"Yes, love has taught us to mellow out on the little things." I said. "We are able to appreciate what each of us brings to our relationship."

The day we married, Allen gave me a heart-melting wink before he kissed me. I recalled how in some ways my childish desires of a blessed husband came true, and I was given not one but two Prince Charmings.

Behind us, the musicians played and sang, "Only Jesus Could Love You More."

Beth Cantrell writes fiction and family lore books. She facilitates the Vacaville Inspire Group and is on the Inspire Board. This Love story is the sequel to her Joy Anthology story. Beth and Allen travel to Sacramento, Minnesota, and Texas to visit family and friends.

NO GREATER LOVE

Sami A. Abrams

Afternoon light filtered through the living room streaking a glare across Michael's picture. As I stood in my dress blacks, cap tucked under my arm, the guests' low chatter at his visitation swarmed in my ears. My eyes caught the folded flag next to his battered helmet. Had it only been a week since the fire? My head was still tender to the touch, and the crimson splotches from the burns on my legs were starting to fade. But I didn't think my heart would ever heal. God had allowed my wife to leave me five years ago and He'd now taken my partner. My best friend. What did I do to deserve this? Tears blurred my eyes. What little I had eaten for breakfast threatened to crawl back up my throat. How could I go on? Michael had a wife and three-year-old son. I had nothing. I was alone in life. It should have been me. Why, Michael? Why? I drifted back to that day.

Flames danced in the windows of the old house. The glow of the full moon illuminated the sky. Trees swayed in the light breeze, but the heat radiating from the entryway made me feel as though I was entering the gates of Hell.

The family stood in the street huddled together. Their six-year-old, Abby, was missing.

Captain Jacobs' voice crackled in my ear. "Make it fast, guys. Do your sweep and get out. This old house is like a tinderbox."

I clapped Michael on the shoulder and leaned in so he could hear me. "Quick sweep, clockwise, and pray to that god of yours we find her."

He slapped my hand and took the lead.

"Abby."

"Abby." Michael's voice echoed mine.

Flames licked the walls, as waves of smoke rolled across the ceiling. My turnout coat took the brunt of the heat, but my skin prickled and stung beneath. I knew our time was limited. Where was that little girl? The thick smoke made seeing nearly impossible. It would take a miracle to find her.

The hiss of breath through my mask resonated in my ears, blocking out everything around me. Captain Jacobs' voice boomed in my ear. It took me a second to register what he had said. "The girl is safe. The house is unstable. Get out now."

Michael spun and together we took off for the entrance to escape the inferno that threatened to devour us.

Ten seconds and we would be at the door. Six seconds…we could do it in four. We needed to do it in four.

A crack reverberated through the house.

Pressure came from behind. Something shoved me through the opening. No, not something, someone. Michael.

Smacking onto the wooden porch, my air tank slammed into me as I hit the ground. My helmet went flying and my mask shifted. I lifted my head and turned to see Michael lying motionless under the remains of the ceiling. A wooden beam laid across his head.

"No!"

Red, yellow, and orange tendrils reached out the door for the back of my legs. Their touch stung.

Smoke curled around me, and the noxious stench snuck under my mask. My throat constricted as it tried to block the deadly fumes. How poetic. I would die just a few feet from safety.

"God, help me."

What was I saying? He didn't care. He never had.

My head thumped back down.

Two hands grabbed me under my arms and carried me from the lethal dragon, as darkness seized me and pulled me under.

A hand lay on my shoulder. Michael's picture came back into focus, and my memory of that night faded away. I didn't turn to face my comforter. By his touch I already knew who it was. Chaplain Torres had visited me multiple times over the last week. I hadn't wanted to talk, so he spent hours sitting with me in silence. I didn't want to admit how much it had helped to know he was there.

Chaps' hand tightened. "He's in God's hands now, Jeremy. Michael's home."

All I could do was nod. Why would I want to know a God who took my partner? But for some reason that night I had called out to Him.

"Jeremy, I'll be gone for a few days with my family, but when I get back please come over anytime. I'm always here for you."

"Thanks." With that, I pulled away and rushed out to my car.

I didn't want to live. How could I go on, knowing my best friend gave his life to save mine?

As I drove through town, I was more certain than ever that living wasn't an option. But Michael had sacrificed himself for me. How could I ignore that? I'd give God one chance to prove He was there.

Moments later, I found myself sitting on the porch swing of Chaplain Torres' house. The sweet fragrance of peonies drifted on the breeze. Birds chirped as they flew from branch to branch. Life went on around me. I would miss the little things. The smell of baked lasagna at the firehouse. The half-court basketball games with the guys. Even my neighbor's obnoxious terrier. But I just couldn't go on anymore. Life was too lonely, especially now with Michael gone.

The sound of a car door caught my attention.

Chaplain Torres walked up the sidewalk with his eyebrows raised and sat beside me, but he didn't say a word.

I focused on the small knot in the wooden porch rail. "I thought you were leaving town."

"So did I. Apparently, God had other plans."

I closed my eyes. Was it really God who sent him back?

He pinched his lips together before continuing. "I was in a hurry and left my cell phone on the kitchen table. I came back to get it. Jeremy, you knew I was leaving town. You want to tell me what's going on?"

I let out a sigh. "Chaps, I planned to end my life today. I didn't want to live with the loneliness anymore. The hurt and guilt are just too much."

I could feel his eyes on me, yet he said nothing.

"I told myself, if you showed up, God really did care and I wouldn't go home and take my own life."

We sat in silence. I didn't think Chaps would ever speak.

"Jeremy, you and Michael were partners. You were best friends. Is there anything you wouldn't have done for him?"

I rubbed the back of my neck. "You know I'd have done anything for him."

"According to the greatest book of all times, there is no greater love than to lay down your life for a friend. And that's exactly what Michael did for you. He knew you weren't ready to die, so he chose to save your life. He loved you, Jeremy."

My eyes burned and my heart ached. Michael had died for me. He had taken that extra second to shove me out of the house knowing he would die.

Chaplain Torres sat in silence leaving me to my thoughts, and I had a lot to think about.

Several minutes later he patted my knee. "You know, someone else loved you that much too. But that's a conversation for another day. Now, I'm going to get my phone and be on my way. I'm glad you were waiting on me. We'll talk more later."

I watched Chaps pull out of the driveway. Yes, I would be here later. A deal was a deal. God had answered my prayer with a stupid forgotten cell phone. It was time to hold up my side of the bargain and give life another chance.

I understood the idea of laying your life down for a friend. I'm willing to do that every day for my brothers at the fire station. But Michael had gone one step farther and had actually done it. Not just for my life, but for my soul. Warmth seeped through my body as Michael's love filled the empty places of my heart. Maybe one day God's love would fill the empty places in my soul.

"There is no greater love than to lay down one's life for one's friends." (John 15:13 NLT)

Sami A. Abrams is an aspiring writer of Christian romance and romantic suspense. She wrote as a summer guest journalist for her local newspaper at age sixteen and is currently writing flash fiction for a sorority Bible study group. Sami has a B.S. in Education and M.S. in Psychology.

A LOVE THAT IS COLOR-BLIND

LR Maddox

"'You must love the Lord your God with all your heart, all your soul, all your strength and all your mind.' And, 'Love your neighbor as yourself.'" (Luke 10:27 NLT)

Do you enjoy eating food? I would assume your answer is, "Yes!" How about foods outside of your ethnicity? Like Italian, Mexican, Chinese, Greek, Japanese, French, or African dishes to name just a few. Again, your response would be, "Yes," right? While I could go on and on about delicious food, the point is we have variety and we savor it. Can the same be said about our relationships? Are they diverse? Do they come from many different cultures?

Scripture talks about loving our neighbors, which involves more than the people who live nearby. The neighbors we are called to love are also at our jobs, schools, churches, communities, and even within our families. These are the people we encounter in our daily life and they are multicultural.

Every nationality is in Heaven, so we should be displaying our love for each other here on earth too. Matthew 6:10 (AKJV) states, *"Your Kingdom come, Your will be done in Earth, as it is in Heaven."* The Merriam-Webster dictionary defines color-blind as, "unable to see the difference between certain colors." We should be forming friendships and relationships oblivious to a person's skin color.

The church I attend is multicultural. Each year we celebrate the anniversary of our church with food, music, and dance from diverse ethnic backgrounds. What a feast for the body, soul, and spirit! This is certainly pleasing to God.

I encourage you to embrace God's color-blind love and ask Him to give you a smorgasbord of neighbors to enrich your life.

LR Maddox is a new writer whose passion is to create works that weave in threads of ethnic diversity, power of God, community, and love. Although not previously published, she is currently writing a novel. Her favorite pastimes are enjoying family, reading, cooking, being a foodie, traveling, and outdoor activities.

Finding God's Love in Dichato
Colleen Shine Phillips

Strings of red, green, and yellow lights dangled over the potholed street where I hurried toward church. A life-sized nativity scene decorated downtown, and English music about snowmen and sleighs blared from speakers nearby. I found that hilarious, considering the temperature smoldered at 90 degrees here in Chile. Sweaty shoppers swarmed the sidewalks, some loaded with packages and others barehanded except for drippy ice cream cones.

I spotted two orange school vans at the curb with boxes of food and donated clothing overflowing from the back. I handed my duffle bag and sleeping bag to the driver, then crammed into the only available seat with my best friend, Manuel, and two other kids, giving a whole new definition to the word close.

"Just think, Eva," Manuel whispered. "If our church had donated three more boxes, we'd have to ride on the roof."

Anita Manriquez, our church youth leader, squeezed into the front seat, balancing yet another box on her lap. "It's a ten-hour trip from Quilpué to Dichato," she said. "So, let's get going."

I leaned over to Manuel as we pulled out of the city. "Have you ever been to Dichato?"

"Not since the quake. I hear they felt it ten times worse down there."

Along with the earthquake, a tsunami had torn many coastal towns in the south to pieces. For months, Chileans had worked to rebuild, raising billions of pesos for those in need. My church sent down supplies every few weeks, and this time they decided to send the youth group with them.

I sighed. "I don't get why they need us to come. Wouldn't it be easier to ship all of it?"

"Come on, *Amiga*, it's only two days until *Nochebuena*. Where's your Christmas spirit?"

"Coming on this trip wasn't my idea. Mom made me go." I reached for my iPod and turned toward the window.

"Can you imagine losing everything and then celebrating Christmas with nothing?" Mom had said. I couldn't imagine it—at least, I didn't want to. Besides, "nothing" had to be an exaggeration. We'd sent food, clothing and school supplies for ten months. That had to make a difference, right?

About halfway through my playlist, I drifted off.

℘

I woke as the vans crawled up a bumpy street toward a sea of wooden houses with slanted roofs. Even in the dark, Anita's face beamed. "We're here!"

We're where? Dichato is—*was* famous for tourism. But I only saw debris and shacks. *How can it still be this bad?*

While our youth leader exchanged hugs with our hosts, we piled out of the vehicles. Everyone collected backpacks and sleeping bags. Except me. I grabbed the driver's sleeve. "Where's my stuff?"

He searched the rack and shrugged. "Nothing else here. Must've gotten left behind—or fallen off."

"It'll be fine, Eva," Anita said. Easy for her to say. She wasn't the one who had just lost everything.

I stood there, wishing I'd picked another shirt for the trip and wondering how I was going to brush my teeth, when a girl about my age came up and greeted me with the customary kiss on the cheek. "I'm Carolina. Come on. You're staying with us tonight."

She took off into the night. Following her proved to be a challenge. Rocks jutted through the sandy path, making it hard to keep my balance.

When we reached the house, I didn't notice the plywood walls or the holes in the ceiling. What caught my attention was the scrawny artificial tree in the corner.

Carolina grabbed my arm and pulled me toward the makeshift table. "Maybe you'd like something to eat? Mamá makes the best homemade bread."

I had a hard time focusing on anything other than what I would wear tomorrow. But southern Chileans were known for their hospitality, and so I didn't want to risk offending her. "Sure." My teeth sank into the hot, crunchy bread. "This *is* amazing."

Between bites, I tried to think of something to say. *Tell me about the tsunami.* No, that would be weird. "So, Carolina, what do you miss most?"

"My stuffed animals, my pictures, my music. Personal stuff you can't get back."

"I'm sorry."

"The tsunami was. . ." She winced. "When the quake started, the earth growled and tossed our house like a feather in the wind. Crouching by my bed, I tried to dig my fingers into the floor to keep my balance, but I couldn't. Then the crashing began—shattering glasses and windows. We gathered up all we could carry and escaped toward the hills." Her voice dropped to a whisper. "All we could do was watch while the monster wave swallowed the town whole—our house, our restaurant, our possessions."

Her words hypnotized me. The earthquake had cracked a wall at our house, and some dishes broke and chipped the ceramic floor, but nothing like that.

As tired as I felt that night, I lay awake for hours thinking about the trip and Carolina and why I was here.

ↄ

Next morning, light stabbed through the window. I sat up, and the first thing that came into focus when my eyelids unstuck was a stack of neatly folded clothes on the end of the bed. Carolina peeked through threadbare curtains into the room. "Hope the jeans and T-shirt fit okay. The public restroom is three houses down. If you hurry, you'll miss the morning crowd."

"Thanks." I jumped up, grabbed the clothes, and bolted for the door. With no shower and no toothbrush, it didn't take long to get ready.

After breakfast, Carolina said, "How about I show you around?"

We made our way toward the beach. About a block from the shore, we stopped in front of two crumbling cement walls. "This was our house." She pointed toward a plot of sand. "And over there stood our restaurant."

I tried to picture her life before the tsunami: going to school, helping her parents in the restaurant, playing on the beach. I wished I could somehow give her a few moments of normal.

Reaching for my iPod, I pulled up one of my favorite songs. Carolina must have recognized it, because she started to hum along before I could hand her the earbuds.

We stayed there the whole morning, listening to every cheesy pop song I had. Sometimes Carolina looked like she was going to laugh, and then sometimes like she was going to cry.

When we got back to camp we saw Anita pulling boxes out of the vans.

"Eva, how about you and Carolina carry a couple of these to her place."

As we stacked the cans and dry goods on teetering shelves, I noticed it was much less than I had thought. With so many people in the camp, two van loads could only go so far. *What if they had to stay here another ten months?*

Carolina's mamá walked in as we finished. She kept wringing her hands while insisting, "Too much, too much," and that only made me feel worse. My mom brought home more than this every time she shopped at the grocery store.

Too soon, it was time to say good-bye. I laid my hand on Carolina's arm. "How much longer do you think you'll be here?"

She twisted her mouth. "Until Papá can find work."

I bit my lip and looked down, only to realize what I was wearing. "Whoa! Sorry, I almost walked off with your clothes."

A dimple formed in her cheek. "Keep them. They're yours now."

"No—"

"Please. You have no idea how good it feels to help someone else."

This wasn't right. I was supposed to be serving *her*. I fished my iPod out of my pocket and pressed it into her palm.

She handed it back. "Thank you, but no. Besides, I know how important it is to you."

"All the more reason."

She shook her head, kissed me on the cheek, and walked away, waving at me.

ဢ

Everybody had room to spread out on the way home. Manuel lay in the back seat, sunburned and snoring. His experience must have been different, because I couldn't sleep at all. I stared out the window at the mountains, so much greener than they were in the north.

Two days ago, I hadn't understood why we needed to go to Dichato. True, we could have shipped the food and clothes, but God wanted more. He wanted me to meet Carolina. He wanted me to see that scrawny Christmas tree, taste her Mamá's bread, listen to music together on the beach. He wanted me to experience His love in a small, tsunami-destroyed town.

We pulled into Quilpué just after midnight. On every street, families gathered to celebrate. Delicious smells filled the air, and different Christmas carols clashed around us.

I thought about Dichato and Carolina again. Now that we were friends, how could I let her go hungry again?

"*Feliz Navidad*, Amiga," I whispered. "See you soon."

This would be the best Nochebuena ever.

*Passionate about God and ministry, Colleen Shine Phillips lives with her family in Quilpué, Chile. Having authored plays, Bible studies, and articles, she has also placed in fiction writing contests. She loves writing short stories. You can read her work in **Clubhouse**, Focus on the Family's magazine for middle graders.*

Boots on the Ground: A Battle for Love

James Burgess

Spit-shining my boots, a futile exercise seeing they would just get scuffed and dirty the next day, I gazed down at the letter I had received from the beautiful Beverly. I had been physically separated from my girlfriend of two years at the hands of the Department of the Army for five whole weeks now. I thought about those fantastic, sparkling, blue eyes, full of love, and a smile that could, as they say, launch a thousand ships to war. Hadn't she, just a year ago, showed her compassion and saved my life by giving me an ultimatum to kick the drugs or else I would lose her love?

The Army decided I should be a leader, because I had some college credits. I was almost three years older than some of the recruits. So, my platoon sergeant made me a squad leader over ten young men, one of whom married at the ripe old age of eighteen. As I looked at my letter, it reminded me of the previous day, when I had to console this same young man who had just received a Dear John letter from his new wife of ten weeks. She had decided she needed aid and comfort from the enemy. The enemy? His best friend. She was running off with him.

I stared at my letter and wondered the same thing, as I reread the lines that tore at my heart. "I miss you terribly, so I went to him to talk and he gave me comfort." Those were the same words from my charge's wife.

How could this happen? Doesn't she say that she loves me with her whole heart, mind, and soul, here at the bottom of the letter where she signed it? I realize she has known him since she was eight years old and he has been like an older brother and best friend to her. But, what about me and my heart now?

I had never known love before, and if this is what it was about, I wasn't sure I wanted any part of the jealousy that came with it.

I decided that in a few weeks when I got leave, I would travel the three hundred miles home and give her my own ultimatum, and a marriage proposal.

Fast forward a year and a half to May 26, 1973. Yes, she accepted my proposal, but not my personal mandate. She continued to talk to him almost daily for advice. I figured I would move her away from her parents, since they were the ones who had introduced her to him. I wanted to have greater influence over her. On the day we exchanged our vows, I hoped he wouldn't show up, but he did. Everyone that knew him loved him, including my own parents and grandparents, but not me. I didn't see what the big deal was. Couldn't they see the division he was causing between us? I was jealous, and here the minister was saying that we needed to spend more time with him in order to strengthen our marriage. Not my marriage, no way! I wanted her all to myself and for her to be dependent on me alone.

Often, I listened to her talk about her discussions with him. My stomach churned. I knew she loved him more than me. *How could she? He is old, and I am modern and young, full of energy.* But once again, she gave me her demands for our marriage to work. *I'm the victim, right?*

We went to his place together, because I wanted to protect her from him. His house was full of people, including my grandparents and the local minister. I became somewhat friendly with the pastor and would meet with him at his office, where we would talk about my wife's and my relationship. However, every time I went, this person, who I didn't care for, would show up. I wasn't as impressed with him as everyone else. In fact, I would say I had come to despise him.

Beverly decided to join the choir and guess why? You're right. There he was, right in the heart of it. For her to participate in choir she had to go to church on Sunday nights for practice. However, I wasn't about to let my wife, who was apparently easily influenced by him, go out at night just to spend time with him. I loved her, and yes, was extremely jealous of her time. I wanted her all to myself and I wasn't going to share with him. That's when I decided I'd go on a reconnaissance mission and find the flaws of my enemy. No way was he going to steal my wife's love and attention from me.

Then it happened one Sunday night, June 1, 1975. The impact he had, even on the minister, hit the peak of deception, in my opinion. I listened to the pastor praise his many virtues. He said many don't know him because they think with their heads and not from the heart.

Am I looking at this from the wrong angle? Have I truly taken the time to fully recon him? Maybe this pastor has the answer, but I'm still going to check him out.

As the choir headed to the loft to begin practice, I sat in my seat and pondered what the pastor had said. *Okay, here is my promise, God. I gathered the facts and I will give him a chance, but I know I won't like him. I'll take the risk to get to understand who he appears to be.*

I stood up and headed to the minister's office to talk some baseball. The Giants weren't doing well that season. I knocked on the partially open office door. The pastor looked up. "Come in, Jim."

The door swung open and I stepped through the threshold and blurted, "I'm lost and I need Jesus Christ in my heart, my life, and my marriage." That's when I realized we weren't alone. There He sat, right beside the minister. They had been conversing. He saw my dark heart, and I saw the truth of His love. He jumped up and ran to me—engulfing me into His loving arms while the pastor sat open mouthed. Now I knew what true love was all about.

That night I talked to my loving wife. "Beverly, I don't care if you love Him more than me. I now understand what I have missed about Him…His love."

After forty-two years, I'm still in the service, but it's His Army now. I'm still a squad leader and I have had many people to lead and comfort. Besides family, there are quite a few who have been loved in our home along the way.

A sharp jab in the kidneys wakes me, as I hear reveille played in my ears with the harsh urgency of an alarm clock. I force open one eye and peer out from under the blanket to see Him sitting on the edge of the bed with His lopsided grin. "Get up. We have skirmishes and battles to fight. Hurry, put on your combat gear. Let's go, let's go, let's go!"

"No." I fight the urge to yell and scream in protest. He knows I have never gone into battle without complaining. I pull the covers back over my head in dissent.

So, He sends in His latest canine recruits, Maxx and Harper, who He has placed into my care. Both are energetic and ready to go. In fact, Maxx has decided it's his job to poke me in the ribs every morning. I grumble in protest as I pull off the sheets, and now He's laughing at me. "Okay," I surrender. "I'll go."

"Will you guys hush. I'm trying to sleep." The beautiful Beverly complains from under the blankets, as one of those sparkling, blue eyes peeks out.

I reach over to slip on my current camouflage fatigues, which are dark blue sweatpants. I grab my boots, which I don't spit-shine anymore, because you don't polish broken down tennis shoes, and I trudge toward the battle field. I grasp my latest weapons, two leashes hanging on a nail by the front door. I move out to war. Then I stop and pause. "I'm not going out there alone, You have to come as my backup if You want any love to come out of this."

We walk out together—me still grumbling—but now listening to His battle plan. He reminds me, I must mow the lawn, sweep the porch, clean up the backyard obstacle course that

Maxx and Harper have destroyed. Harper loves to dig foxholes and she loves to watch me fill them back up.

It's hard to believe that when I got to know Him from my heart and His love, I would fall into deeper love with Beverly and the rest of the world. Who would have thought this jealous, selfish man would wave the white flag and surrender to true love with Jesus?

Jim Burgess is a retired knife-grinder for Molding Mill. He served six years in the Army. He's extremely, happily married to the love of his life, Beverly, for forty-four years. Their grandson, Reese, lives with them along with their furry kids, Maxx and Harper.

LOVE BITES

Dee Aspin

"Can anyone take this sweet dog?" Steve, the ER charge nurse, pleaded again with the staff nurses on behalf of the collarless, gangly pup dumped at the sliding doors to our trauma center.

My heart pounded a little harder each time he rounded through my section of our large ER. Everyone seemed to have an excuse, which temporarily assuaged my guilt.

"I have a dog."

"I don't have a place to keep it."

"My wife will kill me."

"My cat will kill it."

My coworkers had good reasons—unlike me. I simply had not owned a pet in twenty years of single freedom and did not want to be tied down. The last round of the morning, Steve gazed at me steadily, "So...I don't have to take her to the pound in the morning..." He ambled up to me. "If it doesn't work out, bring her back in a week, and I'll take her."

I frowned. "But I'm afraid of getting her in my car." My voice sounded meek, even to me.

"No worries!" John, a husky orderly assured quickly, twirling his stethoscope. "I'll get a blanket and settle her in your back seat…she's a good dog. Probably sixty pounds and less than a year old. The sheen on her black coat is dulled by dirt. Otherwise she appears healthy, muscular, and responsive."

I nodded as everyone but me breathed a sigh of relief.

True to his word, John followed me to my car at the end of shift…with the dog.

"I'm glad I had this old blanket in my car." He covered the back seat of my Civic and tucked it tight to protect my linen seats from the dog's unpleasant odor.

So, reluctantly that morning, a tired, ambivalent nurse drove a quiet, alert dog home in silence, pulled up into the driveway, and shifted gears to park. I turned around and spoke sternly using the name that first came to me on our twenty-minute trip from work.

"Hannah, if you don't let me wash and shampoo you, you cannot come into the house." Hannah's ears perked up. Soon, she stood erect and still, as I poured half a bottle of my shampoo on her coat and hosed her down on the driveway. I scrubbed her and tried to lean back as far as I could, extending my arms and aiming the hose…as not to get my face too close to hers.

The next morning, I took Hannah on a walk. She suddenly lunged to run, and I flew down and hit the pavement on my palms—hard. The road rash stung bad. I shifted the gears with my fingers later that day when I drove Hannah to her first check-up. The vet said she was around nine months old, a Lab mixed with Rottweiler or Doberman, probably because of her clipped tail.

"Too bad you didn't get her younger…she's a bit big for you."

He was right. Hannah was strong and assertive. The second night I had her, she startled me from a sound sleep. She barked and made strange noises. I decided someone else would be a better candidate to raise her. She scared me. I found out Steve was off for a week, so I began asking others if they could take her. Someone needed to train her…before she bit me.

"Why do you want to give her up?" a kind doctor asked me the night I returned to work.

"She makes this deep sound from the bottom of her throat and wakes me up at 2:00 A.M. I look at her, and she's standing at the end of my bed staring intently at me and eyes aglow, and… making those noises. It really frightens me…I don't know what she wants."

"Oh, she just wants to play!" the attending assured me with a smile.

I was surprised. "Well, I'm afraid she's going to bite me." I defended my crumbling case.

"No," she laughed. "That's just the way they try to talk to you." Given the information, my fears lessened. The next night she barked, I tossed her a toy and…kept her. I grew to love her.

☙

Years passed. The next time I pulled in the driveway with a canine in the backseat, it was pleasant. The seven-week-old yellow Lab pup from a ranch whimpered occasionally and carried a delightful puppy smell.

That first night I brought him home, he started biting me as a twenty-pound puppy. Thank God, he wasn't 120 pounds yet. After a few days, I decided he would be difficult to train, because he kept biting me, no matter how many times I taught him, "no bite." That is, until I gained perspective from my patient.

"My dog gives me love bites every day," the experienced Lab owner boasted, when I complained to him in the recovery room about my yellow Lab pup.

"I thought he was being disobedient." I told my patient, and explained how I tried to teach him not to bite.

"There's a difference between biting and love bites," he explained. "Biting is intentional and you would know it because it would hurt. Love bites are gestures of affection."

"Oh…" I rolled my eyes up and put my head down.

I thanked God for that patient and for the people he brings across my path who bring me new awareness. I stopped scolding Sam, and he bit me as I laughed and rumpled his ears, until the day he ran over the rainbow bridge.

And so, we learn in life, as we grow in experience and awareness, how to live with different animals and what their nonverbals mean. It is much like how we learn to live with different people. And usually, it's at the expense of another dog, another kid, another friend, or significant other, that we have learned the things we *now know*—understanding that helps us to care for, react to and love those around us in a better way.

> *Be completely humble and gentle; be*
> *patient, bearing with one another in love.*
> (Ephesians 4:2)

Thank you, Lord, for those in my past, those you placed in my life to learn from. Thank you for the lessons taught, the growth, and wisdom you gave me through the struggles and often misguided efforts done in my ignorance. Help me move beyond the regret and mistakes I've made and move into the grace of growth you've given me now. May all my yesterdays be used for good today for those with me now, and bless those who have taught me, the hard way, for their love.

> *Dee Aspin, inspirational writer, speaker, and Coach, authored **Lord of the Ringless**, **The Dating Dock**, and **Dogspirations**. Her devotions and stories can be found in compilations by Barbour, CBN, Revel, Guideposts, and Inspire. After twenty years ministering to singles and the JJC Chaplaincy, Dee resides in Sacramento with her husband and miniature schnauzer.*

Love Bites / Dogspirations 2015, Inspire Press

God's Text Messages

Rev. Susan A. Cosio

She ran to the mirror to look at her own reflection.

"Really?" she asked with disbelief and a flicker of hope.

I had stopped by the dry cleaners to drop off my weekly pile of dirty blouses and slacks. When the middle-aged woman behind the counter greeted me, I noticed her new haircut, and complimented her on how pretty she looked. She got so excited she dropped my bag of clothes and zipped across the room to stand in front of a full-length mirror. An immigrant from Korea, her English was awkward and broken, but her smile was quick and broad.

"I am?"

I smiled and thought to myself. *Yes, you are. You are beautiful. You are important. You are loved.*

As a hospital chaplain, I have learned the value of a caring presence and a few kind words. People facing life transitions or a scary diagnosis are often unnerved. They feel alone. Abandoned. Afraid. They wonder where God is, and if God is there for them. Their tears or anger may reflect the same fear we see in the disciples in Mark 4. As the storm waves crash around them, they wake the sleeping Jesus in the back of the boat.

"Teacher, don't you care that we are going to drown?" (Mark 4:38 NLT)

Martha expresses similar angst when she feels overwhelmed by all she needs to get done, without any help from Mary.

"Lord, don't you care that my sister has left me to do the work by myself?" (Luke 10:40)

The psalmist begs God to take note of his suffering. *How long, Lord?* he asks, *Will you forget me forever?* (Psalm 13:1)

Even Jesus cries out to his Father from the cross, *"My God, my God, why have you forsaken me?"* (Mark 15:34 ESV)

When we suffer, the sense of isolation and betrayal can be profound. When a close friend of mine lost her teenage son in a tragic boating accident, she told me her deepest fear was that she and her family had been abandoned—even forgotten—by God. I also met a young AIDS patient who asked for the chaplain at midnight when I was on call. Alone in a hospital isolation room, struggling to breathe and afraid of dying, he asked me if God would reject him, the way his parents had. I held his hand and assured him God would not.

Often, patients ask questions that have no easy answers: Why does my child have cancer? Where was God when my husband took his own life? Why does God allow so much suffering?

The metropolitan hospital where I work is in the center of an increasingly diverse city, not far from the state capitol building. Patients come from various cultures, faiths, and life experiences.

They speak different languages and use various names for God. Some are gang members, and some are members of the Assembly or the Senate. Most have not been to church or temple in years.

But crisis often leads people to think and ask about God. I don't always have answers to their questions. But I've learned from the story of Job and his friends that explanations are not always helpful anyway. I am confident of the things they most need to hear:

No, you are not alone. Yes, you are important. Yes, you are loved. And yes, God will be with you, no matter what happens.

We know from the biblical story of Hagar that God is a *God who sees*. (Genesis 16:13) God is a God who comforts and weeps for His people. Psalm 34 tells us, *The Lord is close to the broken-hearted and saves those who are crushed in spirit.* (Psalm 34:18) Sometimes, God uses *us* to draw close to the hurting and crushed.

I believe my primary call as a chaplain is to be an ambassador of God's love: a tangible sign to those who suffer that they are not alone. I am not their source of hope and love, but I can be a harbinger of hope. I wonder if that may be true for all of us. We all have lonely people who cross our paths—in our work, and in our communities. Those we encounter may need to see the light of God or the love of God in our eyes. Not all who are hurting are in the hospital.

Patients and families often cry when I pray for them, deeply touched, but less by my words than by God's presence made real to them. They eagerly (if awkwardly) offer me their hands as if reaching for connection. I cannot cure their diseases, or promise them the outcomes they desire. But I can be present so they are not alone. Sometimes, I can help people access hope. At other times, I just sit with them in the dark. But a shared moment and a few kind words can make a difference in how they frame their experience, and how they perceive themselves.

My husband, Gib, and I have been married for over thirty years. We've raised a family, and we both have demanding and often stressful jobs. But recently, we've found a new way to express our love and support. We text "TA" to one another at random times during the day. It is an abbreviation for *Te Amo*, Spanish for *I love you*. It takes less than a minute to send this message, but it can change my countenance as well as my self-perception. No matter what I am facing, I am reminded that I am loved. That someone is thinking of me.

People who are in pain need reassurance that they are loved. They yearn to know that they are not forgotten or overlooked. In her prayer, *Christ has No Body Now But Yours,* St. Teresa of Avila tells us that we are *God hands…God's feet…God's eyes of compassion.* What if we are also God's "text messages" of love to a hurting world?

❧

Rev. Susan A. Cosio is an ordained pastor in the Evangelical Covenant Church and a full-time hospital chaplain at Sutter Medical Center, Sacramento. She and her husband Gib live in Davis, CA.

Behold Love

Cecille Valoria

Dawn breaks:
God's palette unfolds for all to see,
hues ascending and descending,
in melodic harmony.

A brand-new day commences:
a new beginning,
a turning of a leaf,
in the page of our life.

Of a purpose,
set before the world came to be,
as the seconds tick in precise accord,
He molds each detail.

A forgiveness of blunders done,

covered in the waters,

and no longer resides,

even in a mist.

"Open my eyes, O LORD," I pray,

"that I may behold the love

You have for me."

You are Love.

As seasons come,

and seasons go,

Your Presence remains,

and Your love stays.

Cecille Valoria is an elementary school teacher who loves to journal, write, and blog. A woman of many interests, she indulges in traveling, cooking, and photography with her husband, Sal. Her passions include studying God's Word, praying, admiring His creativity, and spending time with family and friends.

Love So Unconditional

Chrissy Drew

This is how God showed his love among us: He sent his one and only Son into the world that we might live through him. This is love: not that we loved God, but that he loved us and sent his Son as an atoning sacrifice for our sins. (1 John 4:9-10)

Christ laid His life upon a cross at Calvary to save us, mortal sinners, to remove our sins by His blood. A sinless man did this for a sinful world—then and now. Can you even begin to comprehend this?

Unconditional love. Who else has this?

Mothers. Mothers do.

I'm one. My sacrifices weren't as huge as Christ's, but I certainly made sacrifices along the way. And still do.

Once we become mothers, our lives are no longer our own. As a matter of fact, when we become aware of the pregnancy, things change. Our diets, our moods, and our love begins to grow, before we meet our little miracle and look into their eyes. God's gift to us.

Christ was the same way with us. Before we were born, He loved us. He knew us in the dark place of our mother's womb. He knew the color of our hair, eyes, and how we will live and He knows how we will die.

We may not know the future as He, but there were times my boys thought I was a magician for knowing what they were going to do before they did it. The ol' eyes-in-back-of-the-head magic. Or intuitions when I felt they were in trouble.

My situation, when a single parent, was difficult. Two growing boys. Each with different needs. One as sensitive as his mama, the other independent and strong-willed. I loved/love them both, I just loved/love them differently. Not one more than the other—just loved to fit their personalities. There wasn't and never will be the perfect book on raising children—other than the Bible. Faith must be strong.

It wasn't long before I realized their differences would last a lifetime. They would go their separate ways. The battle was no longer mine. Hearts broken that only God can mend.

The love a mother has for her children is a bond never to be broken. No matter how difficult situations get or curves life throws our way. This four-letter word is tiny but fierce. It never diminishes, even if the person is distant. Prayers of a mother for her children go directly to God's ears. They are constant and continual. No matter what.

God put this love in our hearts. His love. He lends us our children for a short time. To care for, nourish, love as He has loved. They don't come with instructions on every personality, experience or era. We learn as we go and grow with each other. We aren't perfect, no not one of us. Have I made mistakes? Of course, and I've learned from them. Will they make mistakes with their children? Most definitely, and I pray they will learn from them, as well.

I know the love they now have in their hearts for their children. They are raising them well. They have morals and respect. I must have done something right.

I know God does not like divorce, but I firmly believe, had their biological dad been in their lives, they would not have turned out as grounded as they are. Each with their own beliefs, but fully devoted fathers and husbands. I'm proud of them. And, if I were to have stayed in a loveless, abusive marriage, I don't think they would have this type of love-lasting marriage.

I have heard of so many families lately who are going through issues with their adult children. Satan is on the move. But, as Jesus pronounced, He has overcome the world. (John 16:33) Greater is He within us than he (Satan) that is in the world. (1 John 4:4) Satan has no chance to deceive us from the love we have for our children. Don't you dare allow him to do so. Be strong and courageous. (Joshua 1:9)

(I don't know about you, but I hate having to capitalize the enemy's name.)

Just as God's love is unconditional. We may disobey Him or His word, we may sin one way or another—we are all sinners and fall short of His glory, but His love is unconditional to those who love Him.

Even though this family may be temporarily broken, repeat— temporarily, my love remains unconditional. It will always and forever be.

No greater love than from our Father in Heaven. None. Zip. Nada. For He loved us first, before we were born, He'll love us until we meet Him as we ascend into Heaven.

Put your faith in Him. Even if you have to love your children from a distance, God loves you and them right where you / they are. He knows your heart. The heart He filled with so much love. Never lose sight of this love—or His. Imagine His arms held out wide. He's saying, "I love you this much."

Amen?

Chrissy Drew lives in Northern California with her darlin', Mike. Although recently retired, she works part-time for a non-profit. She loves writing, gardening, and being the domestic CEO of her homestead. When it's baseball season, Chrissy may spend way too much time watching the San Francisco Giants. Visit her at: chrissydrew.com.

KATHY'S STORY

Suzi Kneedler

Out on the front porch, five-year-old Kathy played with her doll. She looked up when the door opened and her mom's husband stepped onto the landing. He put a key into the lock, twisted it, turned around, walked down the steps and across the street. She stood to watch him until she couldn't see him anymore. She walked to the door, touched the doorknob and began to turn. It refused to budge. Crouching down against the porch wall her young mind raced. *Why did he lock the door? I don't want to be alone. Please Jesus, help me.* Wiping a tear from her face, she waited for her mother to return from work. She watched the shadows grow longer and the moon grow brighter.

Her mom walked up the sidewalk. Ethyl's eyebrows raised as she looked from her daughter to the screen. She unlocked and opened the door and they both stepped inside. Picking up a paper from the table, Ethyl shook her head, turned and walked into the other room closing the door behind her. No hug for her young child. No explanation. No words.

❧

By four years old, Kathy learned about divorce, when her parents split up. Ethyl then married an artist who didn't like being around kids. After only a year, he walked away from them, leaving Kathy outside on the porch. Soon after, Ethyl married another man. With each marriage, Ethyl changed her and her daughter's last name, though the men didn't adopt Kathy. Convenience drove the decision. Using whatever name her mother told her to write on her school papers, left this little girl feeling lost and confused.

These men didn't seem to care anything about Kathy. The artist left her alone on the porch. The next one slapped her face and whipped her with a belt. He would use his belt on her, especially when he had too much to drink. It usually happened when Ethyl left for a weekend leaving him to care for her daughter. From early after he married Ethyl, Kathy learned how to interpret his habits and moods and stay out of his way. Many times, he would take her to the bars with him. Even as a young child, she felt resentment towards her mom for leaving her with him.

Ethyl would divorce, marry, divorce, and marry again with no explanation or conversation with her daughter. Kathy felt like her mother had greater interest in keeping these men happy than in caring for her child. This deepened the feelings of resentment and invisibility in their relationship. It appeared that her mom looked for love in empty relationships marrying men who didn't care about Ethyl's daughter. At least Kathy thought so.

Mom and daughter went to church and did devotions together. Kathy figured her mom loved her but she felt closest to her when they sat at the piano together playing and singing songs.

It just didn't happen often enough, because her mother either worked or focused on her current husband—whichever one lived with them at the time.

Kathy always loved her father. At fourteen, she made the decision to take back her father's name. It made her happy to have a name she wanted. Kathy Willcox sounded better to her than any of the others. Spending summers and holidays with her dad became a break in her otherwise invisible life. He treated everyone with kindness and gentleness, very unlike the other men in her life. She figured if it got too bad at her mom's house, she could always escape to his house. Though her dad didn't go to church, her stepmom took her.

In most areas of her life, consistency stayed out of reach. But no matter who Ethyl married, where they lived, where Kathy went to school, she always attended church whether with her mom or stepmom. She felt at home among the people she knew and loved there. As a teenager, dealing with weight issues caused feelings of invisibility. Those who knew and loved her at church didn't seem to notice her heaviness. They treated her the same way they treated everyone else. She loved the friendships she had at church and felt cared for there. They included her. She felt seen.

Thanks to the love from God's family, Kathy never felt the need to act out or demonstrate any kind of frustration because of the imbalance in her life. It never entered her mind to blame God for her pain and loneliness. She loved going to His house. Songs of praise filled her heart and overflowed into music she composed and played on the piano. She ignored the craziness around her by writing songs to God. She found solace playing the piano because it brought comfort to her and a feeling of safety. She let her emotions come out as she played.

Her first year in college, a sophomore by the name of Ed entered Kathy's life. They immediately became friends. She wanted to keep the relationship on a friendship basis. Due to what she had seen in relationships her mother had, she didn't want a deeper relationship with any man. She had no interest in getting married because she didn't want to follow her mom's example and end up in a failed marriage. But, as she grew to know Ed, she saw a difference in him. She saw a temperament like her father.

By the end of her first year of college, Ed asked her to marry him, and she agreed.

Now, nearly sixty years later, they have two lovely children. Still involved in church, Kathy shares her wit and music with everyone who has the blessing of knowing her.

Kathy often wonders why innocent children suffer for someone else's actions. But through the ups and downs, the resentment toward the adults in her life, and the feelings of invisibility, her faith in God's love remained her lifeline. When God blessed her with such a loving and committed husband, she knew God's plan had come full circle proving depth of love rises above the challenges of life.

(By Kathy LeFranchi, as told to Suzi Kneedler)

Suzi is a retired teacher. She and her husband attend Fair Oaks Presbyterian Church in Fair Oaks, CA. Her passion is to speak the truth in love through her characters in her stories. She greatly admires the 19th century Christian novelist George McDonald.

LOVE BROKE THROUGH

Terrie Brown

See what great love the Father has lavished on us, that we should be called children of God! And that is what we are! The reason the world does not know us is that it did not know him. (1 John 3:1)

When I think of God's love, I can't help but think of this verse. It became a very important verse that God used in my life in an unexpected way.

I grew up always wishing I could be a daddy's girl. My sister got that role, and I never really felt close to my father growing up. It may seem silly, but I always felt this empty place in my heart because of that. I'm a practical person. I just decided that would be an empty place that would always be there. As an adult, I could live with that.

One year I went on a retreat and several people who had been praying for the retreat kept saying God was going to heal me. I felt hopeful that God would move in my heart that weekend, and since I had a knee injury, I hoped for physical healing as well. But God had a better plan. He did heal me, but not in the way I expected.

On the last night of the retreat, while we were praying, one of the ladies came up behind me and laid her hands on my shoulders. As the woman prayed for me, she quoted 1 John 3:1 over and over. God used her prayer to break through a wall in my heart that I hadn't acknowledged was there for a long time. I began to weep as God flooded me with His love. He literally lavished His love on me in that moment of prayer. As He did, I felt that empty place in my heart fill up with love.

I didn't realize I still had that childlike desire to be close to my dad. But God knew, and He chose to heal my pain. Until then, the only other time that I'd felt that much love and freedom flood my heart, happened when I became a Christian. However, during the retreat, God's love broke through the walls, the pain, the empty places in my heart and filled them to overflowing with His amazing, healing love.

It's no mistake that God uses the word "lavished" in this verse. I think of lavished as a waterfall washing over me. The weight of that water nearly knocking me off of my feet. In reality, God's lavishing love is even more than that, because not only did God heal my heart that day, He healed my relationship with my dad. By my releasing that deep-rooted desire—and the pain that I hadn't acknowledged—God enabled me to build a real relationship with my dad. From that moment, God's love that He lavished on me began to flow through me to those around me.

This is God's way. He pours out His love on us so that we can pour out His love on others. His love can heal the deepest pain and emptiness in our lives. Pain, we've decided we must live with, can be replaced with His love, grace, peace, and joy.

Oh, Father, You have lavished Your love on us so many time. First, when You chose to save us from our sin. Your love overcame everything standing between us. Now, You lavish Your love on us to heal the hurt, the emptiness, the injuries that the world and others may have caused. In these, Your love heals and mends and then spills over to reconcile relationships. Because of Your love, we can love and forgive and walk in joy. Father, I want to dance and rejoice in the waterfall of Your love. Let it refresh my soul and open my heart. Let Your love break through any walls I've built to protect myself. And please, let Your love break through to others around me. Thank You for loving us so much and for calling me Your child. I am a Daddy's girl after all. In Jesus's name, amen.

As a pastor's wife, mother of four, and former missionary, Terrie Brown has been writing about faith and knowing God through her experiences raising kids and living in other cultures. A teacher at heart, her desire is to grow closer to God and show others how to do the same.

McKenna

Janell Michael

She stole my heart the first time I looked into her deep blue eyes. She was only minutes old, but already she had me wrapped around her little finger. I loved her from her peach-fuzz head to her fat fingers and toes. She was our angel on earth. When McKenna was in a room, her presence filled that room, almost to the point of taking your breath away.

One of my favorite memories of McKenna, at about age three, was the day she found some worms in our garden. Oh, how she loved those worms. I'll never forget the look on her face when I told her they would have to stay in the garden because they were just too dirty to come inside. Well, that didn't stop McKenna. When I wasn't looking, she quickly stuffed them into the pocket of her overalls.

As I was preparing lunch, she was happily cleaning up in the bathroom, or so I thought. When I went to check on her, our sink was full of suds and worms! McKenna was in the process of shampooing them after she had given them a bath. Luckily I stopped her from turning on the blow dryer to finish the job!

If I could go back, I would never have made her take those worms back outside. I would have found a box for them or some other container, anything, just to keep that smile on her face. Not long after the worm incident we found out that our McKenna had a very aggressive form of leukemia. From that moment on, most of our time was spent in the Children's Hospital at her bedside. No more days of washing worms. Gone was her messy pigtails and round plump baby body.

The thing about McKenna was she could still command a room. One smile would wash away all my sadness and fear. She would look into my soul and promise to be with me forever. She'd pat my hand and ask about her worm friends she loved.

In her heart I think she knew she was leaving us soon. On that last morning together, I held her in my lap stroking her back. With her last breathes she sang to my husband and me "Jesus loves me this I know. For the Bible tells me so. Little ones to Him belong. They are weak but He is strong." She looked up with a smile and closed her eyes. That song will forever be in my heart as much as my lovely daughter, McKenna.

*This is Janell's first year as part of the Inspire Christian Writers' family. She has great hopes that her first book **Fairy Tales Redeemed** will be published within this next year. Janell lives in Northern California with her husband, David.*

THE NEXT BEST THING

Debbie Jones Warren

Let the morning bring me word of your unfailing love,
for I have put my trust in you. Show me the way I should go,
for to you I entrust my life. (Psalm 143:8)

The moon shone bright in the African sky the final night of my junior year at Hillcrest High School in Jos, Nigeria, where I lived in a hostel with forty other MK's (missionary kids).

"I have always wanted to marry a man I've known my whole life, someone I grew up with," I confided in my roommate Eileen, as we lay in our beds chatting after lights-out.

"But how are you going to do that? Tomorrow you will leave your home, the town, and this continent!" Her whisper rose a faint octave as she puzzled over my improbable notion.

Shaking my head, I exhaled a deep, soft sigh. "I have no idea." Soon we both drifted off to sleep.

The following day, my family and I left the country where I had lived most my life. My parents, missionaries with SIM (Serving in Mission), raised five kids in West Africa. Beginning in first grade, I attended boarding school five hundred miles north of our home for eight months each year. I only lived with my parents on their rural station for summer and Christmas vacations. Those lengthy separations were overwhelmingly lonely for me. Consequently, having the foundation of a long-standing relationship with the man I would marry was paramount for me.

Because we were scheduled for furlough, I needed to leave Nigeria and move to an unfamiliar land for my senior year, to the place my parents called home. In the San Francisco Bay Area, I slowly settled into high school and the youth group at our church in Oakland. Numerous members who supported my parents' ministry looked out for us when, every few years, we returned to California on home assignment. One family was especially supportive the year I was in fifth grade, hosting us often for dinner and putting the seven of us up for a few nights when we needed transitional lodging.

They had a daughter my age, Carole, as well as two sons a little older. Carole and her brother Chris invited me to bowl in a league with them, and no one minded that I threw a gutter ball nearly every frame. With his long straight hair and aviator glasses, Chris reminded me of one of the Beatles.

He invited me on a few excursions that year, including a day with the family at Santa Cruz Beach Boardwalk. While I enjoyed his attention, I didn't feel attracted to him, and I still dreamt of marrying one of the many boys I had a crush on in boarding school, now a continent away. After graduation in June, I left for college in Fresno, and heard that Chris started dating a girl from church.

At Fresno State, I went out with a few guys, but I always was a little uneasy because they felt like strangers, even though I had known them at school or church for months or even years. I didn't know their families, and that was important to me, since my family situation while growing up was disjointed. What was more, I wanted my date to know something about the land where I grew up.

The summer after my first college year, I flew back to Nigeria to visit my parents and siblings. I looked out for single, eligible friends, but no reconnection surfaced, and I finally let go of that unrealistic dream.

About that time, I began driving back up to the Bay Area monthly in response to an invitation by Carole from my old church. She announced her engagement and asked if I would be a bridesmaid. I was delighted to renew our friendship. Each time I visited, her brother Chris was at home, and with a shorter haircut and stylish glasses, he looked cuter than he had several years prior.

The big weekend arrived. After the rehearsal dinner, Chris was my partner to practice ballroom dancing. He was a great dancer. However, when he waltzed me across the floor, I stepped on his shoes. He pretended not to notice.

At the reception, Chris played a flute solo for the bride and groom. After the piece was done, he slipped into his seat beside me at the head table.

"You play like a professional." I smiled sideways at him.

He clasped my hand under the table, and I felt his arm trembling. In front of the crowd he appeared so poised and self-assured, but I realized his confidence was only external. My heart went pit-a-pat.

After the celebration ended, he gave me a ride to my aunt and uncle's house. Chris closed my car door, then rounded the back of his timeworn, yellow station wagon. As I watched in my sideview mirror, he leaped up in the air and kicked his heels together. At this I was hooked. The guy was a gentleman and he acted delighted to be with me.

That evening, Chris entertained me with stories about his family history, in which I now had a keen interest. Born in Scotland, he immigrated to California with his family after he turned five. Every year his family and his relatives in Scotland traveled back and forth to keep in touch.

He confided in me how much he still loved Scotland and wished his parents had stayed there. "I always hoped to one day marry a bonnie Scottish lass," he said with a cheeky grin.

Then I revealed to him, "I used to dream of marrying one of the guys I knew when I was a kid on the mission field, so I would be familiar with his family and background." I went on to share stories of my life and friends in Africa.

After chatting a while, we realized that because Nigeria had been a British colony, I was familiar with countless Scottish words and concepts. I knew that potato chips were called crisps, a cookie was a biscuit, and a truck was a lorry. As we discovered that we also shared many similar experiences with international living, a warm and fuzzy glow enveloped me like a comfortable blanket.

Two weeks later, Chris drove to Fresno to take me to dinner, and we started long-distance dating. In May, he and I graduated from college one week apart, and a few days later he left with his buddy Jim for a six-week European backpacking trip. I mailed two newsy letters to Scotland so he wouldn't forget me.

On his return, we discovered the separation had drawn us closer. Chris joked, "I guess you are the next best thing to a Scottish lass for me."

Remembering I had first met him at church at age ten, I retorted, "You're the next best thing to someone I've known my whole life."

On Christmas Day, I looked for an engagement ring under the tree. When a glittering diamond didn't materialize, I swallowed my disappointment. Unbeknownst to me, Chris wrote to my parents asking for their blessing. However, international mail traveled by freighter at that time, so he had to wait two months for a reply.

In the spring, I drove up to help the family decorate for his sister's first wedding anniversary, even though I felt puzzled they were making such a big deal out of it. Prior to the party, Chris hired a limo and took me to a sumptuous brunch at the Claremont Hotel to celebrate our one-year anniversary of dating. On the drive, he pulled a jewelry box out of his pocket, displaying a ring he had chosen himself.

In the center of the band a perfect diamond twinkled, with three successively smaller diamonds stretching out in a row on either side. Even though I had often imagined a swirled setting, I loved this ring because Chris spent time and effort selecting it.

He smiled and asked, "Will you marry me?"

Sniffing back happy tears, I knew without a doubt my answer was "Yes." I clasped my arms around his neck, and the long kiss we shared sent a cool tingling down to my toes.

After brunch, the limo delivered us to the Warren's home, where I found I had decorated for my own engagement party. As we entered, fifty people jumped up and shouted, "Surprise!"

My eyes turned into a waterfall when I realized my three brothers drove hours to celebrate with us. On our wedding day in March 1985, I thanked God for His remarkable provision of a lifelong friend for me. In the ensuing thirty-two years, Chris and I have grown to feel we are a perfect fit. We still marvel at the wonderful way God fulfilled both our desires to marry someone with a connection to our respective homelands.

Every so often, Chris and I joke about how we each settled for the next best thing.

Born in Alameda, Debbie Jones Warren grew up in Nigeria with missionary parents. She lives in Castro Valley with her pilot husband, Chris. She loves spending time with her three astonishingly brilliant young adult children and her exceptionally talented daughter-in-law. Her favorite hobbies are collecting china tea cups and hosting teas.

THE EXERCISE

Julie Blackman

As I walked towards the library building, all I could think about was what am I going to write? I entered the double doors and veered to the right to return a book at the return drop station before walking into the library. Even though I arrived later in the afternoon, it was still busy. I scanned the room to find a quiet area to write. Ahead of me were tables by the window facing the lake. As I got closer, I could see at least one person seated per table. From the expression on their faces, they wanted it to remain that way. Off to the left of me, was a nook with one row of four chairs, a table, and a computer. I'd been to this library several times and never noticed this area until now.

After plugging in my laptop, I sat down, closed my eyes, and said a little prayer. *Dear God, please imbue me with Your wisdom and reveal to me what to write.*

Immediately, I could hear an inner voice. *Take thirty-seconds and write down every word that comes to your mind about the love of God.*

What a great idea. I reached into my handbag and pulled out my cell phone and set thirty-seconds on the stopwatch. Instead of jotting down a bunch of words, I found myself pausing to think about how I've seen God express His deep love for me. When the buzzer finally went off, I had ten words listed.

Trust. God can be trusted. He is sovereign and His timing is perfect. I may become impatient at times and expect things to work out in a certain way, in the least amount of time. But God is not a genie. So as time passes, I am taught to be patient, praise Him while I'm waiting, and trust God. Sometimes, through the waiting period, He'll show me events that He protected me from. Other times, I get to see the extent He will go to cover me. Therefore, I can only come to one conclusion: His way is the best way for me.

And those who know Your name will put their trust in You; For You, Lord, have not forsaken those who seek You. (Psalm 9:10 NKJV)

Strength. How many times have I claimed that I can't make it? It's too much. Yet, God continues to give me the strength to carry on. From the moment I wake up, He funnels a spiritual boost of energy to keep me going. Then I realize, I can make it through. When I am weak, He makes me strong. His grace is sufficient.

I can do all things through Christ who strengthens me. (Philippians 4:13 NKJV)

Kindness. I feel God's lovingkindness encompass me every day. He is compassionate and guides me to His Word for encouragement. He reminds me that He is in control. Nothing happens to me without His permission. He supports me and bears all my burdens, if only I would turn them over to Him.

Because Your lovingkindness is better than life, My lips shall praise You. (Psalm 63:3 NKJV)

Helper. I can count on God. There is nothing too difficult for Him. Setting up appointments are not necessary. I can call on Him any day of the week, at any time, and He is always available. When God intercedes on my behalf, I know all is well.

God is *our refuge and strength, A very present help in trouble.* (Psalm 46:1 NKJV)

Comfort. Not only is God my Master Helper, but when I need comforting He is there. I remember a day when I prayed for God to take away the pain that I was experiencing, and I felt a warm presence envelope me. I knew He heard my prayer. Within minutes I felt at peace.

He heals the brokenhearted And binds up their wounds. (Psalm 147:3 NKJV)

Shield. Some days it feels as though I've been on the battlefield. But because of God's shield is protecting me, I am a conqueror. His Word warns me to put on the whole armor of God so that I can stand. And I know that I do not stand alone. I have angels guarding me, and He watches over me day and night.

Yet in all these things we are more than conquerors through Him who loved us. (Romans 8:37 NKJV)

Life. If it wasn't for the love of God, I wouldn't be here today to testify of His love towards me. He gave me life and made it possible through His Son, Jesus Christ, who shed His precious blood on Calvary to ensure I go to Heaven someday. It was a very costly price to pay. I am glad I accepted Him as my Lord and Savior. He makes my life worth living.

For God so loved the world that He gave His only begotten Son, that whoever believes in Him should not perish but have everlasting life. (John 3:16 NKJV)

Hope. If you don't have hope what do you have? I may not know what my future holds, but I am assured that God has a plan for my life. Therefore, I build my hope on the solid rock of Jesus Christ and know I don't have to fear.

For I know the thoughts that I think toward you, says the Lord, thoughts of peace and not of evil, to give you a future and a hope. (Jeremiah 29:11 NKJV)

Joy. When I am sad, God makes me glad, and I can smile knowing that in the end God is going to work all things for my good. Therefore, I don't have to wait, I can rejoice now.

Rejoice in the Lord always. Again I will say, rejoice! (Philippians 4:4 NKJV)

Friend. God is the best friend I could ever have. He promised to never leave me nor forsake me. I can give all my cares to Him and He shows me how much He cares for me. He means the world to me. And of course, He made the ultimate sacrifice by sending Jesus Christ to Calvary for me. What a precious friend I have in Him.

Greater love has no one than this, than to lay down one's life for his friends. (John 15:13 NKJV)

God demonstrates His love in various ways. I hope you enjoyed reading this piece. When you have a moment, try this exercise for yourself. God's love transcends human understanding. We may think we know how deep God's love is, but we only comprehend a minutia of His tender, unconditional love. I can love others, because He first loved me. Thank you, God, for loving me!

Julie Blackman writes fiction short stories and nonfiction inspirational pieces. She thinks words are precious and the biggest loss is to not share them. She considers writing a privilege and desires to be a writing instrument for God. Her work is published in **Inspire Victory, Inspire Promise, Inspire Forgiveness,** *and* **Inspire Joy.**

THE MOST DIFFICULT WAIT

Ron Chin

Perhaps the most difficult aspect of waiting on God occurs when a person feels that God is absent. Although God promises that He will never leave or forsake His children (Hebrews 13:5), people may experience times when they don't sense the presence of God. Jesus experienced this when He went through the horrible crucifixion and waited to die:

Two rebels were crucified with him, one on his right and one on his left. Those who passed by hurled insults at him, shaking their heads and saying, "You who are going to destroy the temple and build it in three days, save yourself! Come down from the cross, if you are the Son of God!" In the same way the chief priests, the teachers of the law and the elders mocked him. "He saved others," they said, "but he can't save himself! He's the king of Israel! Let him come down now from the cross, and we will believe in him. He trusts in God. Let God rescue him now if he wants him, for he said, 'I am the Son of God.'" In the same way the rebels who were crucified with him also heaped insults on him.

From noon until three in the afternoon darkness came over all the land. About three in the afternoon Jesus cried out in a loud voice, "Eli, Eli, lema sabachthani?" (which means "My God, my God, why have you forsaken me?"). (Matthew 27:38-46)

Jesus experienced the most difficult wait. He suffered from not only the physical pain of crucifixion but also the shame from religious leaders and ordinary criminals. The magnitude of the pain and suffering caused Jesus to feel that God had forsaken Him.

Why did God allow Jesus to suffer through such an awful death? Jesus could have just been executed quickly without experiencing the terrible anguish of waiting to die on the cross. However, Isaiah 53:10 tells us that *it was the Lord's will to crush him and cause him to suffer.* God had a purpose for Jesus' life—to die for the sins of humanity so that people could be restored into a loving relationship with God. Jesus' suffering showed that He carried the burden of all the sins of humanity, and demonstrated His great love for people. If someone goes through tremendous suffering for your benefit, then you know that person really loves you. The terrible anguish that Jesus experienced when He waited to die shows the magnitude of His love for us.

In addition, Jesus was the ultimate example of a person who demonstrated perseverance. The author of the letter to the Hebrews wrote:

…let us run with perseverance the race marked out for us, fixing our eyes on Jesus, the pioneer and perfecter of faith. For the joy set before him he endured the cross, scorning its shame, and sat down at the right hand of the throne of God. Consider him who endured such opposition from sinners, so that you will not grow weary and lose heart. (Hebrews 12:1-3)

If you are waiting on God and do not sense His presence, continue to seek Him and remember the great example of Jesus, whose difficult wait demonstrated His great love for you.

Prayer

Jesus, thank You that You love me so much that You were willing to go through the most difficult wait on the cross. Thank You for enduring the most terrible physical, emotional, and spiritual suffering so that I could be restored into a loving relationship with God.

Ron Chin worked in high-tech for over ten years before answering God's call to ministry. After completing a seminary degree, he served as an associate pastor in San Francisco for almost six years. Ron lives with his wife Jill in Fremont, California.

Excerpt from *Waiting on God in a High-Speed Culture*, Xulon Press, 2016

You Love Me Still
Heather D. Blackman

You knew I'd go astray,
But You love me still.
Abandon Your way,
But You love me still.
Had moments of shame,
But You love me still.
Lived life like a game,
But You love me still.
Deep in transgression,
But You love me still.
Yielded to temptation,
But You love me still.
When my actions have a cost,
You love me still.
When my witness is lost,
You love me still.
When I make life a mess,

You love me still.

You love me no less,

No, You love me still.

Won't give up on me,

Because You love me still!

Heather D. Blackman is honored to share her creative spirit through her passion for writing poetry. Her poems have been published in **Inspire Promise**, **Inspire Forgiveness,** *and* **Inspire Joy**. *It is Heather's desire that her poetry will uplift, encourage, and express the love of our Heavenly Father.*

HUMAN-SHAPED HOLES

Robynne E. Miller

I've wondered all my life what draws people together.

My childhood best friend, Gabby, wasn't a thing like me: Hispanic, a dimpled beauty, from a solid two-parent home, and Catholic. I had pale skin, freckles, rolls of chub, a fractured family, and a complete lack of exposure to any sort of faith. But every summer, for the best part of ten years, neither of us knew how to navigate the long, hot days if we weren't glued to each other's hip. And then there was Scott, my dearest male friend from my high school days. Despite the differences in our genders, our vastly different approaches to life in youth (me: obsessively serious, him: carpe diem!), and the incredibly divergent paths, which have often separated us by six thousand miles or more, his brood and mine have remained close over the last several decades. Closer, I would say, than family. And, of course I can't leave out my husband: funny, intelligent, kind, and, in my opinion, gorgeous. But I've known a whole lot of smart, funny, good-looking men who didn't elicit tummy flutters or mild bouts of depression at every separation.

But how did these relationships form and flourish? Why does one person remain on the periphery of our lives while another is imbedded permanently into our hearts within moments of meeting? Why do two seemingly identical people pop into our worlds, one remaining always a bit of a stranger, the other instantly becoming the sister or brother you never had? Why?

Every time I think of this, a 1980's reproductive education video pops into my head: a grainy clip of zillions of little swimmers hurtling through the dark toward a distant egg in a desperate, instinctive attempt to get there first. Dozens seemed to arrive all at once and began nosing along the outer wall of the egg, hoping to be the one chosen for absorption. Despite appearing identical in almost every way, only one, or, rarely, two, ever found their way inside. The facts of life, we were told.

It's like that with us, isn't it? Most of us are pressed on all sides by humans, through family, through work, or through school. Through our interests, communities and churches. But only a precious few slip through our outer shells and become absorbed into our inner beings, our DNA, mingling for some important stretch of time or even forever.

In my mid-twenties, the week before my husband and I met, I had a little conversation with God. I'd decided that I could be happy as a single person, if that was the plan, but if a husband *was* in the cards, I thought laying down a few ground rules would be prudent. He couldn't be 5'11" or have dark hair, for example. Or have that annoying cross-country runner physique which only served to emphasize my stocky roundness. Oh, and, most definitely, he must be local. (Long distance relationships are HARD!)

I thought that was a reasonable list…not too exclusive or picky. And clearly born from a careful assessment of the men I had always seemed to go for and never ended up with permanently.

Enter my beloved Ian. Black hair, 5'11", a lithe long-distance runner and, get this, almost exactly six thousand miles from my home in Northern California to his in Suffolk, England. Everything I never wanted, and more.

Yet within moments of "meeting" through work, and despite being only typed words on a screen, both of us, we admitted months later, knew that our lives had changed forever. Six months after our first introduction, and months after the work project had ended, Ian walked off a plane for what was supposed to have been a two-week, completely platonic "visit." We were engaged a week later, married a year after that, and celebrated our twenty-first anniversary last spring.

I'm still trying to figure out how all that happened.

There was a lot of publicity about our relationship in the UK. Brits were about a decade behind the US on matters of the Internet, with very few homes even having a personal computer. So, the whole country was trying to puzzle out how we could have met, connected, and fallen in love with each other from that distance and through that medium. TV show hosts, documentary directors, magazine writers, and newspaper reporters kept asking us how on earth we did that. I never could articulate a satisfactory answer, for them or for myself.

But twenty plus years is a long time to ponder an issue and I think I've figured it out. I guess I never felt like I "met" Ian. Or Gabby. Or Scott. It was more like *remembering* them. Like opening your closet and discovering a long-lost pair of favorite shoes or a sweater your treasured grandma knitted for you years before: they were there all the time, just waiting for rediscovery and to be brought out into the light.

When exploring my own faith in my late teens, I often heard about a "God-shaped hole" in our hearts. The idea is that there's an inherent void in our lives, to be filled only by Him, which keeps humans seeking truth, purpose, and meaning until we do.

I like to think that there are similar holes in our hearts shaped like every single person we are meant to be in significant relationship with. And, though a million other similarly shaped people might press in against us, only the exact, right ones slip through the outer shell and into the piece of our hearts they were always designed to occupy. That's why it feels like remembering them. They were always a part of us; we were just separated for a while and only needed to click back together.

My unlikely friendship with Gabby was for a season. We drifted apart by junior high, when she went to the local Catholic school and I went to the public one. Her family moved to Colorado sometime later, and I never heard from her again. But I love her, still. And I'm grateful for the childhood we shared and explored together.

Scott's family and mine have both settled back in Northern California, only three hours apart. That's a bit of a miracle after his military tours in Iran, Iraq, Afghanistan, and Saudi Arabia, and my time on the east coast and almost ten years in the UK. We don't see each other every day, but are in constant contact. Each time we're together, it's as if those thirty years never saw us separated for a moment. He's my brother in a very, very real and powerful way.

And, of course, I remain utterly entwined with Ian. Despite my initial "ground rules" and outlined expectations, my journey with this foreign, dark-haired runner was always designed to be long and profound, and the adventure thus far has not disappointed. I'm glad I waited for him. I'm glad God didn't listen to me. I'm glad I didn't settle for *almost* the right size and shape. Life's a bit of a roller-coaster, and I can't imagine how we would have held on if we weren't snapped snuggly into our pre-designed places in each other's hearts.

Though I still wonder what draws two people together and what exactly signals that "this is the time and this is the person," I no longer worry too much about it. People connect or they don't. For a short season or a lifetime.

And I love the thought of that…the mysterious expectation of that. So, I keep my eyes up and open, ready to welcome those precious few I will need to remember and love in the future.

Robynne has authored eight books and numerous articles and essays. She serves on the Inspire Board of Directors as Director of Leadership, leads two critique groups, and is a thesis defense away from her MFA in Creative Nonfiction and Fiction. She's married to Ian and is mom to four amazing kids.

LOVING MY CHILDREN TO OBEDIENCE

Laura Dorsey

As I was spending time with God one morning, He spoke to my heart. He told me that I was teaching my children to perform for love just as I had been taught.

At this time in my life, I was homeschooling four children of varying ages, personalities, and learning styles. A new baby was added to our family almost every two years while living far away from all relatives. On top of all that, my husband had recently started a new business. I was overwhelmed! My life seemed like mission impossible on many occasions. Dealing with attitudes from seemingly ungrateful children made me feel unappreciated.

On days when my emotions led the way, it was an absolute fiasco. My meltdowns seemed like a volcano waiting to erupt, and occasionally it blew. Whenever one of my children's behaviors was unacceptable or inappropriate, I sometimes yelled at them, walking away frustrated and angry with tears falling down my face. Have you felt this way?

Growing up, my family did not often address our conflicts verbally. We would distance ourselves in the conflict by our body language or silence. This was my way of protecting my heart and punishing my children. Teaching performance-based behavior to my children did not start with them. It started when I was young as I looked for love and acceptance after my own parents' divorce. I created my own version of parenting based on my experiences. If I was still simmering and my children came to apologize and ask for a hug, I would say, "Not right now!" I had allowed my peace and joy to be taken away.

On this particular morning, God pointed some things out to me:

- I was allowing the enemy to make my children feel rejected.

- I was making them perform for my love.

- I was not displaying self-control.

- I was giving their unacceptable behaviors control over me.

- Most of all, I was not loving them to obedience.

Can you relate to me? Have you reacted in a similar fashion?

Well, this story is not over yet and there is hope. Through God's great love, grace, and mercy, He guided me to a better path. First, God reminded me of the ways He parented me, much differently than how I treated my own children. His arms were always wide open to love me regardless of my bad attitudes or self-proclaimed pity parties. God showed me that the path to love and obedience was through His goodness. It is never based on what we do, but on the very fact that we belong to Him.

Or do you despise the riches of His goodness, forbearance, and long suffering, not knowing that the goodness of God leads you to repentance? (Romans 2:4 NKJV)

Let me share some of the steps I have taken to love my children to obedience:

• Even while I am still simmering, I embrace them with a hug and talk to them about my feelings and then let them share about their feelings with me. This was hard to do in the beginning, but as I have grown in His grace and forgiveness, it has become much easier.

• I reassure them of my love. I want them to recognize their behavior is not who they are. My love is not based on their performance.

• It's important to ask them to forgive me too. Just because I am the parent, does not make my response the correct one in every situation.

• We pray together over the situation. It allows God's wisdom and healing into our relationship.

God wanted to teach me how to parent as He does out of an unconditional love. No matter how much I may fall short, my Heavenly Father's arms are always open wide. My goal is to show my children the same love, discipline, and obedience that He has shown me.

But God demonstrates His own love towards us, in that while we were still sinners, Christ died for us. (Romans 5:8 NKJV)

Laura and her husband, Vance, live in Northern California with their seven children, whom they've homeschooled for almost fifteen years. She is a member of Inspire Vacaville Critique Group.

DO IT FOR DAD

Analiese Bondar

A warm breeze rustles my short hair as I watch the short, green grass dance in the wind. I release a deep, content sigh and continue reading in the shaded protection of the old oak tree. Its branches stretch out, making me feel like I am engulfed in a big hug whenever I am under it.

"Michelle. Come for dinner!" Mama calls from the porch. I grab my book and run home. Mama's dinners are the reasons I love evenings so much. Another reason why I adore evenings is getting to watch the sun set and the stars come out under the old oak tree with my favorite friend, my dog, Aubree.

I run up to the porch and sit down. I can smell the sweet aroma of beef stew—my favorite. My mouth waters when I grab a fork to dig in, but Dad says, "Not a chance, Apple Blossom. Go wash your hands in the mudroom first."

I sigh, but quickly head towards the mudroom because the quicker I wash, the quicker I'll be able to eat. While washing, I look at myself in the mirror. The green-eyed, short blond-haired girl stares back at me. I giggle. There's a smudge of mud on my cheek from when I explored our creek for the hundredth time. Maybe that's why it's called a mudroom.

I skip happily to the table and plop down. We say grace and start to eat. Conversation bounces around the table like a cheerful bunny. It's mainly the usual. "How is school, Michelle?" "Did you finish that project?" "Did you have fun outside today, Michelle?" Dinner seems to be going fine until Mom asks Dad how work has been. He works for a landscaping company a couple blocks from our farm. This question is nothing out of the ordinary, but something's different today.

"Nothing happened," Dad says.

"What do you mean?" Mom asks with her fork hanging in midair.

"Nothing means nothing. Now can we please finish eating?" Dad's voice sounds stern and angry. I wonder what's wrong.

"Well, it doesn't sound like nothing." Mom's voice rises.

I look at the two of them. *This isn't a good sign.*

"Darn it, Barbara! Can you just drop it?" Dad almost never calls Mama by her name. He is yelling now and his face is completely red as a ripe tomato.

"What is it, Matthew? What happened to make you this mad?"

"You wanna know why I'm mad? I'm mad because I had to q-u-i-t from my j-o-b! Now I can't support you or Michelle and it is all because of my—"

He stops talking. Tears cascade down his face in silent rivers. He puts his head in his hands.

Mom gasps and runs to his side. "I'm sorry," she says.

"Me too," he replies.

Mama gestures towards their room. Dad nods and they both leave to, as they say, "discuss the matter at hand." All I hear are the words "quit," "fainted," "leukemia," and a lot of sobbing.

I gasp. *My dad had to quit? He has leukemia? He fainted? Are we going to have to move?* So many questions run through my mind. Tears slowly trickle down my cheeks. I grab my dog, startling her, and rush into my room. I cry on my bed for hours and wait to hear from my parents.

At 11:00 p.m., I head to the kitchen for a drink. Mama sits at the table which still has the dirty dinner dishes on it. Mama's face is in her hands, as she shakes her head. She looks up at me, surprised.

"What are you still doing up? I thought you were in bed."

"I'm thirsty. Where's Dad?"

"He's in bed resting. I'm sorry all of this is happening. Are you all right?"

"I'm ok, I guess. What happened?"

Mama takes a deep breath. "Your father fainted when he was mowing a lawn today. Last month he found out he had leukemia. Today, his boss said he had to let him go. It isn't safe if he continues to faint and put himself at the risk of serious danger. Your dad and I talked it over, and we have to move into the city where he can get better medical attention."

I gasp and think to myself. *Leave home? I've lived here all my life. The rolling brook, the old oak tree, the farm. Everything is so special to me. How can we leave?*

"I know it's hard, Sugar," Mama pats my hand. "But it's worth it. If we do this, Dad will get better."

I sigh. "Okay." I say goodnight and return to bed. My only thought: *I'll do it for Dad.*

℘

It's been four months since we moved to the city and Dad is getting better every day. I am so thankful for the love and support I get from my new friends at school. And I try to give that same love and support to my family because they are the real troopers, especially my dad. I often look back when I heard the news that we had to move. I remember Mama said it would be worth it. And it was. Since the move, Mama has a great new job. Dad is getting so much better. And I have an amazing new school and new friends. I now realize that if Dad needs anything, even if it means we have to move again, I'll do it for him.

> *Analiese Bondar goes to a Christian school in Northern California. She loves hanging out with her friends and family. She also loves spending her time drawing, writing, and playing with her dog. She wants to become an animator someday. She also loves books.*

LOVING TRUST

Missy Vigil

The first six months of my life I spent in a foster home;

My teenage birth mom had second thoughts, not relinquished, so I was alone.

Facing the inevitable, she finally relented and let me go;

She avoided the family disowning her, nevertheless an agonizing blow.

My new parents brought me home dressed in all pink, their hearts relieved and thrilled;

An incredible blessing, but adoptees can have emotional needs that may go unfulfilled.

With closed adoptions there are no answers to basic questions kids ask naturally;

I'd often wonder, *How much did I weigh? Did I have hair? What's my nationality?*

A life dream is to look at someone with the same eyes, facial expression, or the same grin;

But I never searched for my birth parents and chanced feeling rejected all over again.

Being adopted created an emptiness like the first chapter missing from a book;

No way to be rewritten, it's just not there, as if stolen by a thieving crook.

What filled in was a sense of loneliness and sadness, I didn't understand why;

Many times, I was fearful, a little depressed or so angry I would just cry.

Leading up to and through every birthday I've had over most of the years;

Triggered deep feelings of abandonment and struggles to fight back the tears.

Consequently, most of my life I've spent waiting for the other shoe to drop;

Relationships don't last, people always leave, I'm helpless to make it stop.

An important fact about these two issues I will try to explain as I reflect;

Emotions from my adoption and feelings for my parents run parallel, never to intersect.

In other words, God's gift of loving parents gave me a strength I otherwise wouldn't have had;

The innate deep sense of loneliness was created by a circumstance unrelated to Mom and Dad.

God began filling that emptiness when He planted my own family tree;

My three children and three grandchildren acquired traits inherited from me!

As an adult, I'd say one of my biggest issues is a lack of trust;

God redirects to show me following Him is an absolute must.

With a series of events still emerging in God's perfect plan;

I am seeing it is only through Him that I will be okay with who I am.

Throughout the last few years, He has zeroed in on showing me;

Growing in His Word with faithful obedience and focusing on Him are key.

But in recent months His message is pointed specifically;

Only He is in control, so trust in Him completely.

Trust, my inner struggle, why is it so hard to always do?
Trusting makes me vulnerable, it's risky, causing fear I can't work through.

This was now the time for clarity, the Lord made it known;
The truth is I will never work it through, I cannot do it alone.

But He is lifting me over those stumbling blocks with Divine determination;
I will trust and will not be afraid; for the Lord God is my strength and my song, and He has become my salvation. (Isaiah 12:2 ESV)

The ways the Lord changed my heart, if only I could paint a picture for you to see;
Let me articulate one example of something that happened recently.

It was this past Thanksgiving when we realized the day on which Christmas would fall;
We could spend it at our cabin in the mountains and have a white Christmas, after all.

I immediately checked the weather forecast for that area on my phone;

Oh no, Christmas week? "All sunshine," and all I heard were sighs and moans.

This is the one chance we've ever had to be in the snow on Christmas Day;
With God our Father there are no limits, so bow your heads and pray.

It is now two weeks before Christmas when I checked the weather report again;
And there for December twentieth was a snow forecast where none had been.

Another week goes by, as I continue to pray and my family cannot believe;
The forecast says it's supposed to snow the twenty-third as well as Christmas Eve!

My youngest daughter Taylor, my best friend Donna, and I left for the cabin for a mini-vacation;
We could enjoy two days before starting with all the holiday preparations.

We had no idea as we slept throughout the very first night;
We'd wake up to surrounding trees, cabins, and grounds all covered in white.

Donna and Taylor sat in awe that He answered our prayers while we were asleep;

I explained, "When we pray according to His will, God hears His faithful sheep."

Later on, as we trekked through the snow searching for a Christmas tree;

A posted travel warning caught my eye, the anxiety now multiplying in me.

Heavy snowfall continuing throughout tonight, chains required from Murphy's on up;

My husband Kim and our son Beau, driving up tonight and neither has chains, *now what?*

I try to call and text, neither responds, then I'd soon come to find out;

Not enough room for our German Shepherds, they're forced to take two cars, *by which route?*

Into Big Trees Market we go for groceries, I'm praying for a weather change;

We emerge to discover it had stopped snowing, it was now only rain.

I giggled to myself thinking, *That was fast,* and Taylor asked me why?

I told her what God did, and now we both had tears in our eyes.

Hours later, snow falling hard, it was anything but clear;
I return to my Father's throne for comfort, to suppress any fear.

Heavenly Father, can it just stop snowing until Kim and Beau get here? Please help them out of this bind;
Okay Missy, first you want snow, then you want rain, snow is okay, but not till later? I sound out of my mind.

At the time, we did not know when either would arrive, in retrospect it was thirty minutes before;
The snowing ceased, the roads cleared, now no chains were needed for sure.

My husband arrived safely and I hugged him tightly then, he shared concern for our son;
As I looked at him, I heard myself saying, "I choose to trust in Him, I believe He's got this one."

Within minutes, Taylor walked to the front porch, up the stairs came the dogs and her brother Beau;
So thankful they arrived safely, then Taylor shrieks, "Mama, come here, look!" Yes, it started to snow!

Tears stream down my face as I watch the snow fall, God is speaking directly to me;

He's been leading me, over the past several months, towards a truth He knows I need.

In that moment, overcome with emotional sobs, I realize God's offering something I've never known;

I am here Missy, Trust in Me always, I love you and will never leave you alone.

Look beyond to see this is not about what God gives me through my answered prayer;

At the heart is our loving and merciful Father filling the needs to end despair.

This hinges on the immeasurable power of our Almighty God who knows what we need, when we need it.

To His right sits our Redeemer Jesus Christ, whose blood has given us the way out of that fiery pit.

Yes, we all fall short of the glory of God and yet, our Divine Creator wants us for His own;

He provides everything we need, so recognize His Supremacy and kneel at His majestic throne.

While my words lack eloquence to illustrate our Eternally Sovereign and Most Holy One;

I forever give thanks and praise where it rightfully belongs, to the Father, the Holy Spirit, and our Lord and Savior, God's Son!

Every birthday for the last ten years has been completely free of any emotional pain related to my adoption!

Commit your way to the Lord; trust in Him, and He will act. (Psalm 37:5 ESV)

> *Missy is happily married, with three children and three grandchildren. She began writing in college, but her degree is in dance. She owned a dance studio and spent about twenty years teaching, choreographing, and producing shows. Currently, Missy teaches in children's ministry, studies God's Word in Leader's Council, and writes.*

LOVE IS KIND
Frieda Yang

It was 1962. China was going through a great famine. Under Mao Zedong's zeal to transform the country from an agrarian economy into a socialist society, China went through a rapid industrialization and collectivization. However, this Great Leap Forward campaign yielded the greatest death toll in human history, estimated at twenty to forty-three million people. Food was scarce.

Due to the harsh political campaigns aimed at the rich, Father had been jailed for one-and-a-half years for being a factory owner. He left China for Hong Kong, without telling Mother that he was never coming back.

Mother was only thirty-two. Never having graduated from high school or worked outside the home, she shouldered all the responsibilities of raising five children aged fourteen to just a few months.

One of my first recollections of Mother was seeing her chew a mouthful of peanuts and then transferring it to my baby sister's mouth. With not enough mother's milk and no baby's formula available, she mixed rice cereal with soymilk for the baby.

Ever since I was old enough to help Mother in the kitchen, I would see her nibble on scraps, bones, and chicken feet. But she saved the good meat for us.

"Eat," she'd say when we sat to lunch. Our main meal for the day was plenty of green vegetables with plain white rice. And she would ration a spoonful of stir-fried shredded pork to each of us. If there was any left over, she served herself. Sometimes, the meat and vegetables ran out. Then, we just used soy sauce to flavor the bland rice. Breakfast was a bowl of watery, thin rice gruel, and so was dinner—served with heavily salted pickled radishes, fermented tofu, and sometimes a small amount of fried peanuts.

More than once, I saw her *not* eat at the family meal. "Aren't you eating?" I'd ask.

"I am not hungry," she'd say, smiling.

When everyone finished, I collected the dishes and followed Mother into the kitchen. I saw her scrape up the bits of leftovers, using a little rice to wipe clean the sauce—wolfing it down. She'd let us finish first then only eat the leftovers, away from us!

On my birthday, Mother fried me an egg and made it clear to everyone it was for me. Then, she asked me to buy some fresh noodles—for eating long noodles on one's birthday symbolized a long life.

Spicy food was her favorite. But my weak stomach could not handle it. She always cooked a separate portion of non-spicy food for me.

Saving the best food for us was not the only thing that made a strong impression on me. Saving all resources was her rule in the house. "Just this much is enough," she'd say. She would show us how to squeeze a little bit of toothpaste instead of covering the whole length of the toothbrush. Without central heating and hot water in the winter, we always soaked our feet in a basin of boiled warm water before bed. She would say, "Don't throw away the water. I'll use it right after you."

Always hungry in the afternoon and seeing friends having cream crackers, I asked her, "Can we buy some crackers for snacks?"

"We don't have a budget for snacks. But I can make some." She then used sweetened dough and made what she called, "flag cookies."

When it was the Mid-Autumn Moon Cake Festival, I asked her again, "Could we get some mooncakes?"

"Hmm…let's try making them ourselves." She made the sweet red bean paste first, and then filled little dough balls with it, flattened them, and baked homemade "mooncakes." They were not the best-tasting cakes, but I felt so loved by her, I savored them nevertheless.

After seeing the distance Mother would go to try to make me happy, I learned not to ask her for store-bought food again.

Mother's kind heart extended to anyone who came to her for help. When her former housemaid knocked on the door to ask for work, she just handed her some money despite our tight budget.

A doctor friend asked Mother if she could take in for a while an Indonesian Chinese lady recuperating from kidney disease. She was a university student and had no family in China. Without hesitation, Mother took her in and never charged her a penny for room and board for seven years.

A few years into the Cultural Revolution (1966-76), many students who had been sent to the countryside as farmers returned to the city to escape a harsh life. One such young man came knocking on our door.

"Aunty, do you have small jobs for me in exchange for food?" He was the son of an acquaintance.

"Of course. Go to the back door to the garden. I will give you some work," Mother said.

I was puzzled at Mother's actions, knowing how little we had. After she closed the front door, I said, "But Mother, we don't have extra food…"

"Never you mind. You see how thin he is? If we can, we share. I'll find something for him." Mother went straight to the kitchen.

I let the young man in through the back door. He looked around and started sweeping the yard that looked clean to me, since I swept it twice a week myself.

In a while, Mother came out with a big serving bowl full of food. "Come, eat. Work later," she said

He buried his face into the rice bowl as though he hadn't seen food for days. Mother gave me a satisfied look. It warmed my heart seeing him enjoying the food.

When he finished, Mother said, "You shouldn't work now, not right after eating. Why don't you go home? There isn't much to do anyway. Come another time."

I noticed Mother did not eat for the rest of the day.

In 1974, our family was blessed to be reunited. We immigrated to America in 1976. Mother was forty-six and was blessed with a surprise-son. She continued staying home, taking care of us and the new baby, and never complained.

The church across the street from us was very kind to our family. Seeing how Mother isolated the young boy at home, they offered him free nursery school. She was very grateful to them and became a Christian. She was also grateful to this country for the rest of us, because we were able to attend colleges with full financial aid. "When you are able, always help the less fortunate," she said.

Never having gone to school for English, Mother managed to learn it on her own well enough to pass her citizenship test. Upon naturalization, she gave herself a new name: Mary Young.

With the few people she met and despite her limited English, she would still help others in any way she could.

Once, she saw a neighbor running up and down the street, calling franticly, "Billy! Billy!"

Realizing the neighbor couldn't find her little boy, Mother went to search the wooded section of the backyard. She finally spotted little Billy, sleeping in the neighbor's thick bushes. She called out loudly to the neighbor over the fence, "He is here. Billy is here, sleeping!" She was glad to be able to use her English.

The neighbor was so grateful. She kept thanking Mother.

In her late seventies, Mother's domestic help, a new immigrant from China, Lady L, was worried she would not pass the English test for her naturalization. Mother took up the task of teaching her—taking long walks with her, practicing English conversations—all the while paying her for "cleaning" the house as she was hired to do.

When my mother passed away, Lady L traveled a long way to be at the funeral. With tears, she waved a U. S. passport at Mother's closed eyes. "See, Sister Mary, I passed the test. You never gave up on me and kept encouraging me. Thanks to you I am now a citizen!"

I found among Mother's possessions a notebook filled with Christian songs and articles. Some were written by her and published in a Chinese newspaper. These were evidence of her connections to the Lord, with songs of thanksgiving and praise. Among them was a page with a verse copied in both Chinese and English:

Do not let kindness and truth leave you. (Proverbs 3:3 NASB)

I knew whenever Mother wrote anything in English it was because she wanted all of us to be able to read it, including our youngest brother born in this country. No doubt this verse summarized who Mother was, a self-sacrificing mother with a never-ending lovingkindness. Kindness is infectious. One gesture at a time, a kind seed can reap a bountiful fruit of kindness, rooted in God's love, as it is said in the Good Book, "Love is kind…" (1 Corinthians 13:4).

Frieda is a violin teacher and lives in Granite Bay, CA with her husband, Richard, and four children: Thomas, James, Madeline, and John. She came from China when she was a teenager. She enjoys writing and testifying about the power of God.

HIGH ON THE HILL, BEYOND THE STREAM

Elaine Faber

Praise God, the mother lives and the child is born. "See me, I am here at last." A father sheds tears of rejoicing for the son who has been given, dismissing the pain and fear that held the household captive until dawn. He plants a tiny oak seedling on that morning, high on the hill, beyond the stream, giving back to the Creator a peace offering, a love offering watered with thankful tears of gladness. "We are whole. A son is given, and all is well. We are a family."

❧

A tiny lad stands by the sapling as the sun glints against a new fallen snow. He reaches as high as he can and puts a paper star on top of the tiny tree. The father remembers three years of springs and summers, winters and falls, planting and harvesting. He rejoices anew at the joy this child brings to his life. The Christmas star sparkles in the sun as if to give a silent hallelujah and acknowledgement of the miracle of life.

❧

The lad lies beneath the tree, gazing into the stars that wink and blink across the endless sky, into the myriads of planets and galaxies beyond. The young tree sways in the evening breeze, and a tiny leaf falls onto the boy's face. He twirls it between his fingers. As he drags it back and forth, feeling its caress across his cheek, he wonders at the majesty of God.

❧

On another day, the youngster pulls himself into the tree, climbing higher and higher, hiding deep in its branches, while his father calls his name. A task undone, a broken vow, and grim retribution stalks below. The boy crouches to hide beneath the canopy of leaves. A struggle ensues, as he ponders the consequences of his thoughtless deed. *Run away, face the punishment. Run away, face the punishment.* A decision made, he calls, "I'm up here, Father."

The father reaches up his hand as the lad climbs slowly down. "Give me your hand, son. If we hurry, we can do your chores together. Mother doesn't need to know."

❧

A young man and his bride stand beneath the sheltering branches of the stately oak, as friends and family gather, their faces wreathed in smiles. "Dearly beloved, we are gathered together to join this man and this woman…"

Father squeezes mother's hand, and an accordion squeals out a tinny rendition of the wedding march. The tree's leaves quiver, as if rejoicing in the love of the couple standing beneath its spreading boughs. A kiss, a shower of rice, and it is done. They are man and wife.

❧

The years pass, good and bad. Children are born, and older loved ones die. Year after year, spring follows winter, as the land submits to the plow. Harvests fail or prosper according to nature's whim. The young man's shoulders grow stooped, and his hair turns grey, as he watches his daughters grow and marry. He works the land with his son and grandsons and knows joy and sorrow according to God's will.

☙

In the fullness of time, friends and family, children and grandchildren gather again beneath the wide and spreading branches of the mighty oak. They come to honor a friend, a father, a grandfather. It is a time of farewell and yet, a time to rejoice and celebrate a life.

Clouds gather. The rain begins to fall, and the people rush closer beneath the shelter of the spreading branches. Lightning flashes. Thunder crashes, and they wonder if it is the voice of God declaring... *Welcome home, thou good and faithful servant...* beneath the tree, high on the hill, beyond the stream, where a tiny seedling once was planted on the day he was born.

Elaine Faber is a member of Sisters in Crime, Northern California Publishers and Authors, and Cat Writers Association. She has published three cozy mysteries, two humorous WWII novels, and multiple anthology short stories. Elaine volunteers at American Cancer Society Discovery Shop and leads an writers' critique group in Sacramento.

A Hero's Love

Alice Klies

He was my hero, my shining star, and the whipped cream on the good life he gave me. "Steadfast," "honest," and "quietly strong" are words and a phrase that describe my daddy. Always a gentleman, I counted on his sound advice and unspoken love to lift my spirits from any sad or troubled event in my life.

Daddy shaped the lives of my brother and me, his grandchildren and great-grandchildren. He taught us the virtues of patience, kindness, a willingness to work hard, and the ability to look at our shortcomings and try to better them.

Every day since my daddy passed away, I feel pride in the legacy he left behind. The essence of his soul lingers in my heart. I feel his presence and hear his voice as I recall memories of him.

When I sit quietly in a backyard rocking chair while marveling at God's creation in the blue sky peppered with soft billowy clouds, I remember how Daddy used to sit in the same chair and point to the clouds. "Oh, look, Alice. See the puppy dog there? Look, his ears look like they're flapping." Then, he would laugh and point to yet another of his imaginary creatures in the sky.

Daddy lived with my husband, daughter, and me for the last ten years of his life. It was truly my honor to care for my daddy until he took his last breath. I knew he loved me even though he didn't often express his love aloud. I also knew without a doubt that my daddy believed in our Lord and Savior, even though, again, he never talked about his beliefs, one way or another.

Imagine my surprise when I went through his belongings, a task most difficult to do, and found a journal full of his precious written words. As I thumbed through the pages, I found the following letter:

"To My Daughter - I Love You

"My day becomes wonderful when I see your pretty face smiling so sweetly. There is such warmth and intelligence radiating from you. It seems that every day you grow smarter and more beautiful, and every day I am more proud of you.

"As you grow through different stages of life, you should be aware that there will be times when you feel scared and confused, but with your strength and values, you will always end up wiser. You will have grown from your experiences, understanding more about people and life.

"I have already gone through these stages, so if you need advice or someone to talk to, to make sense of it all, I hope you will talk to me. I am continuingly cheering for your happiness, my sweet daughter. I love you."

Daddy's letter brought me to my knees. I looked up and praised God. "Thank you, dear Lord, I so needed this." Tears ran down my cheeks. An unbelievable joy filled my heart.

When I was able to control my overwhelming emotions, I continued to turn the pages of Daddy's journal. I found another letter he had written to my brother with many of the same beautiful sentiments of love. I brushed more tears from my cheeks before I came to Daddy's last written page.

God is with me to this day.

He has shown me the way to the beyond
that everyone must face.

There is a time for happiness

and a time for sadness we must all face in our lifetime.

I feel God has left a place for me.

❧

Daddy loved me, and I know for sure our reunion will be sweet in Heaven.

🜊

Alice Klies is President of Northern Arizona Word Weavers. She is published in seven **Chicken Soup for the Soul** *books, fourteen anthologies,* **Angels On Earth**, *AARP, and* **Word Smith Journal**. *She hopes her words will bring a laugh, a tear, or encouragement to someone, somewhere. She is currently writing a novel.*

A FLYING CARPET

Brian David

The calls came in one week. First my dad, "Your mom is not doing well, the cancer makes it painful for her to eat. She is losing weight fast." Then my younger brother's call, "I've been to see mom...she is going fast...I don't think she has much time left. Can you make it home this month?"

I set the phone down. Standing up from my brother's call was like getting up from a blindsided tackle. Every simple sound was amplified—the chirping crickets and the buzzing mosquito, but busy sounds—like the outside traffic—were sedated. Our living room looked basic, complex issues vaporized. Life was simple. My mom was dying. I had to return home.

My parents lived in California, 24,000 miles away from us. In five weeks, my wife was due to deliver our fourth child. Sitting on the edge of our bed, my wife and I talked about the news. We decided I would catch the next flight from Karachi to Los Angeles. My wife and three children would remain in the Islamic Republic of Pakistan.

After making flight arrangements I told Latif, my Pakistani friend, "My mother is dying from cancer. I am flying home to see her." Latif did not speak English; our communication was in his third language, and my second, Urdu. For him, conversing with me must have been like communicating with a two-year-old. But he was patient, he was kind, we connected, we understood one another.

The night before flying out, while tucking clothes into a suitcase, the doorbell rang. I welcomed our guests opening the steel gate, and ushered them through our screened patio into a small living room. Following cultural protocol, I turned to go into the kitchen to start *chai*. A simple visit in Pakistan could lead to sharing a meal and, if the conversation went on, to having overnight guests.

Latif stood up, bidding me to not make anything.

I insisted, "No, please you need some chai."

He insisted, "*nahi (no)*," he was resolute, as he came with a specific purpose. "I brought you something." He went to his friend's car and returned with a rolled-up carpet. He unfurled it in front of me saying, "It is for your mother," then with a gentle smile continued, "tell her it is from your good friend in Pakistan and that I hope she feels better." My eyes clouded, he uttered a phrase in his mother tongue to his driving friend, they stood, bid farewell and walked out, before catching the emotion I was struggling to contain.

Christ floated his love to me and my family through Latif, and his flying carpet remains a fragrant uplifting memory breezing through my life. A carpet that flew over the pain, suffering, and loss was made airborne by love. Love knew my pain. Love came beside me and love bound our friendship beyond words. Love flies above religion, transcends culture, and floats beyond our fallen world. I believe in flying carpets.

BRIAN DAVID

Brian began writing poetry when he was in high school as a way to interpret his world. He wrote character sketches while traveling in the south Pacific, newsletters and feasibility reports while working in South Asia, and human-interest articles while living and teaching in Mariposa, California.

What is the Song of Songs Doing in the Bible?

Deb Gruelle

Rise up, my darling!

Come away with me…

Look, the winter is past,

and the rains are over and gone.

The flowers are springing up…

The fig trees are forming young fruit,

and the fragrant grapevines are blossoming.

(Song of Songs 2: 10-13 TLB)

In the past, Jews forbade The Song of Songs to be read by anyone until they were over thirty years old. The reason for the age restriction? When people are younger, they can be too focused on the world in front of them to understand.

Maybe you remember trying to read it when you were younger and how you ended up joking with your teen friends about the intimate body parts listed in this book. Maybe you even wondered why God would include it in the Bible. Or maybe a Bible teacher brushed it off as simply a picture of marital love.

If you're over thirty, try taking a new look at this book of the Bible to rediscover the allegory depicting God's intense love for us. Especially, if like me, you've sometimes settled into viewing your time alone with God as something to check off your list each day. Reading the Song of Songs slowly can draw you back into the passionate love God intends for your relationship with Him.

This year, at well over thirty, I read it again and finally understood why it's in the Bible. It offers such amazing insights into the depths of God's passion for each of us.

As a writer, I'm also amazed how Solomon bravely wrote this allegory from three wildly different points of view other than his own Jewish male viewpoint. For Solomon to best tell this story of God's love, he stretches to write first from the viewpoint of a woman of a different ethnicity, then from the viewpoint of God, and lastly from the viewpoint of a group of female bystanders. Stepping out of his natural viewpoint enabled Solomon to share unique perspectives and relatable details of his love for God and to lean more deeply into the image of God's love for us as His bride. For instance, this book speaks of reveling in God's view of us as beautiful, a tougher thing to do from a male perspective, but one of God's deep pictures of His love for us. Solomon's example encouraged me to also stretch to try to view God's love from diverse perspectives.

We can develop twisted thinking when we don't fully realize the intensity and completeness of God's love for us. The Song of Songs does nothing less than usher us into the holy mystery of God's personal, passionate, and joyful love for each of us.

So, I encourage you to read the Song of Songs again for the first time. Look for all the ways God delights in everything about you.

Prayer: *Father, thank You for including the allegory of the Song of Songs in the Bible. May we absorb what You want to communicate to each of us through it. May its images of You delighting in us fill us to overflowing so we can then pour out Your love on others.*

*Deb Gruelle, a new Inspire member, has been writing for over two decades. Because she had so much trouble getting her kids to go to sleep, she wrote a children's book, **Ten Little Night Stars** (release date is January, 2018). She also wrote **The Ache for a Child**, for women dealing with infertility.*

A Love Story Only God Could Write

Christine Hagion Rzepka

Little Vic was a four-year-old boy who enjoyed playing with a stickball in the streets of Chicago's Polish ghetto in the early 1950s—a nostalgic time for most, remembered for soda fountains, sock-hops, saddle shoes, and pink poodle skirts. But for little Vic, a Catholic from a poor family, it was the beginning of an epoch.

One evening, when his parents were both working, Little Vic was playing on the living room floor with his Lincoln logs while his babysitter was in the kitchen.

She was not cooking dinner or doing dishes, but was rolling out the twelve knives she'd brought with her, carefully wrapped in a bath towel, concealed in her purse.

"Li'l Vic!" she called out casually, as though calling him to dinner.

He darted into the kitchen, though he knew he was not supposed to run in the house.

Instead of giving him a nice snack, she plunged a butcher knife into his small back.

The preschooler howled in pain as she followed that knife with another, then another. When she finished, his back looked like a well-used dartboard. Blood oozed out of the youngster onto the cold tile floor. His breathing was shallow, and pain overtook him. Suddenly everything went black.

Though his little body was stabbed twenty-seven times, miraculously, he survived. Nine months later, the day finally arrived when he was released from the hospital.

Little Vic's parents took him to Mass the following Sunday. He stared at the stained glass and the gold-gilded scrollwork on the molding of the cathedral, waiting for his moment. He knew his catechism well: God is *omniscient,* a word Little Vic could never quite pronounce correctly. He pondered that thought through the sermon, and when the organ began to play, while others gathered their hats and gloves before exiting, he ran up to the priest in front of the altar.

Father Adrian, greeting his parishioners, felt a gentle tug on his robes.

Little Vic looked intently into the eyes of the middle-aged priest. "Father, if God is all-powerful, and all-knowing, and everywhere present, then why did He let this happen to me?" His innocent eyes pleaded for an answer to the question that had plagued him for nine months in the hospital.

Father Adrian appeared to have no idea how to respond to the existential question of the ages. "I don't know, son. You'll just have to take it on faith."

Following graduation from parochial school, Victor entered Catholic seminary to become a priest, feeling he owed a debt to

God for allowing him to survive the brutal assault. Yet after the first year, the dean told Victor that his feeling of obligation did not equate with a call to the ministry. Victor's puzzled mind couldn't take it in. He shut God out of his mind and heart from that day on.

While others burned their draft cards, Victor enlisted in the military. Inducted into in an elite squad carrying out covert missions around the globe as a Navy SEAL, he'd finally found a channel to funnel all his rage and unanswered questions, and relished killing his enemies.

Who would have thought, in the midst of a guerilla war in the jungles of Vietnam, amid the blood and the sweat and the bugs and fear, that God would be playing matchmaker?

∽

On the other side of the globe, Christy, then in the fourth grade, excitedly prepared for what would be a most eventful evening. Without much to do in her small desert town, when Beulah invited Christy to a Billy Graham Crusade, she readily accepted.

The fiery words of the famous evangelist pierced her soul. Running up at the altar call when the first musical notes began, Christy pledged her heart to the Savior of all mankind. Because Christy's family didn't attend church, she knew little of religion.

After the crusade, Beulah's family explained what it meant to be a Christian over hot-fudge sundaes at the local Denny's.

Christy's life was forever changed. Although her family didn't share her newfound faith, a fire was kindled within her young heart that night that was never quenched.

Christy later became a missionary, fell in love, and got married. But her fairy-tale life was a mirage: the man she'd married was abusive. Believing that Christians should not divorce for any reason, Christy resigned herself to a life she knew was far less than God's best. One night, during a vicious beating, she knew her husband was going to kill her. She lay on the floor, his foot crashing into her ribs. As his large hands squeezed the life from her, Christy breathed her final prayer: *God, I said 'till death do us part.' I don't understand, but if this is Your will for me, so be it.*

Her husband repeatedly kicked her unconscious body, and then went off to a church picnic, leaving her broken and bloodied body for dead.

Surprised when she regained consciousness, Christy was even more perplexed at God's instruction to leave her husband. *But God, what about 'what God has put together, let no man put asunder'?*

The answer she received cleared up all doubt. *You can't do anything for Me if he kills you.* God led Christy to a battered women's shelter and helped her rebuild her shattered life.

Believing her husband's threats to hunt her down if she ever left, she changed her identity. She relocated several hundred miles away, changed careers, and had reconstructive surgery to repair the damage he had done to her face.

Years later, Christy (now Christine) sat in a steam room at her local gym, relaxing after a workout. She chatted casually with a Korean man, YoHan, about fitness, nutrition, and dating in the '90s. Their conversation continued when they moved to the Jacuzzi.

"There is someone I'd like for you to meet," YoHan offered.

Christine began to give her usual refusal when someone tried to set her up, but this time, the Holy Spirit silenced her.

YoHan introduced Christine to his friend, Vic, at an outside coffee house.

Because she had chosen so poorly the first time, Christine had told the Lord years before that she would remain single unless God chose a spouse for her.

Eventually, God made it clear to her that Vic was the one He had selected for her, although he was an agnostic.

But God, she queried, *what about 'Be not unequally yoked together with unbelievers?* Once again, God surprised her with His instruction. *He's not a believer yet, but he will be.* Knowing that she could trust the word of the Lord, Christine obeyed.

YoHan, the best man at their wedding, beamed.

Months later, in the privacy of their living room, Victor bore his soul to Christine about the attack he'd endured as a child, and how he'd turned away from God as a result. Still unable to reconcile his victimization with the concept of an omniscient God, Victor asked Christine the same question he'd posed to the priest. "If God is all-powerful and all-knowing, and everywhere present, then why did He let this happen to me?"

Dumbstruck, she set her teacup on the floral couch, hands shaking. Victor's question was the very same one hidden deep inside her own heart. She prayed, silently. *God, no human can answer that question. The priest caused so much harm with his flippant reply. I need Your wisdom to soothe the gaping hole in Victor's heart.* The response was in her mouth before she had a moment to consider the words. "It's the wrong question," she replied. Then, she panicked, *God, Why did you have me say that? What does it mean?*

Suddenly, images flashed before her mind's eye, as though fast-forwarding through movie scenes:

Li'l Vic running into the street after his ball, a Mac truck approaching inches before his frightened eyes—and an invisible hand picking him up by the scruff of the collar, depositing him on the sidewalk.

Victor as a young soldier, being stabbed with a poisoned bayonet in the Vietnam jungle.

Victor being nearly decapitated by a member of the Vietcong.

Victor as a captured POW, being tied to a tree and used for target practice.

Suddenly, she knew the answer. "Victor, the right question is not 'why did God let this happen to me,' but 'why did God love you so much that He worked so hard to make sure you survived so many times'?"

The question that had haunted them both for years was finally answered in this glorious epiphany.

Through this insight, the accusation in Victor's heart became a search for purpose. Victor's journey led him first to the waters of baptism and into the arms of His Savior, the only One who can heal such deep wounds.

In God's sovereign, unfathomable way, He used one survivor of attempted homicide to minister to another. By doing so, He showed that God's love turns death into life, hatred into hope, and deep woundedness into profound healing.

Christine Hagion Rzepka writes poems, songs, blogs, and books. An ordained minister, she has counseled abuse victims for over fifteen years. "Rev. Red" (her nickname) founded The Lazarus Project to raise awareness of the issue of family violence in the Christian Church. God can heal the wounds of abuse.
www.resurrectinghope.org.

He Chose

Loretta Sinclair

She lost her job, and then took mine—because she was afraid.
I should hate her, but I don't. I chose love instead.

He belittled me to get his manhood back—because he had lost
it. I should feel sorry for him, but I don't. I chose love instead.

She tried her best to control me—because her own life was out
of control. I should do my best to get away, but I don't. I chose
love instead.

He was totally indifferent to me—because that's the only
emotion he knows. I should walk away, but I don't. I chose
love instead.

❧

They all should have loved me, but I never felt it. I only felt
anger, hostility, jealousy, and rage instead. Emotions pushed
down, swallowed, buried for decades…so long they cannot be
found by anyone any longer.

But love is in there somewhere. God put it there.

People do hateful things every day.

Look behind the behavior. Look at the person.

Hate is a choice. So is love.

❧

Judas turned Christ over for thirty pieces of silver.

Peter denied knowing Him three times that night.

Christ was beaten so He was no longer recognizable as human. He was crucified on a cross. Tortured. Humiliated. Murdered.

He could have hated them, but He didn't. He chose love.

He bore my sins upon His shoulders. The hatred and pain of all humanity laid across His bare back. He should hate me, but He doesn't.

He chose love instead.

"Forgive them Father, for they know not what they do."

❧

Christ has felt all our betrayals and hurts. He was insulted, despised, plotted against, blamed, and more, yet none if it was His fault.

His mother and brothers felt He was insane at one point. His best friends turned Him in. His Heavenly Father, the one true and great God of the universe let Him die—alone, so I could choose love instead.

The next time you feel like all is lost, and no one loves you, sit back and smile. He chose love when He chose you.

You're in good company.

A lover of God and lover of words, Lori Sinclair is a single parent, working mom, and both a business and fiction author. Her dream is to retire one day and be a full-time author.

FAITHFUL LOVE

Lori Hartin

Then I will heal you of your faithlessness;
My love will know no bounds...
(Hosea 14:4 NLT)

Two weeks ago, she had promised herself it was over. But that afternoon, in the darkest corner of Araceli's Cantina, they met and ordered lunch again. Their meetings at the Mexican eatery, tucked between a women's boutique and the local pharmacy, teetered between the thrill of stolen moments and the fear of being seen. But she had always assumed the risk.

Irresistible. That's what he was.

Unfaithful. That's what she was.

It had started innocently enough. Thrown together on an investigative project for the local newspaper, their constant contact was easy to justify. She was a local reporter with zero photography skills, and he was a freelancer available for special assignment.

Michael was the perfect find, and a big distraction from her life.

Separated from his wife, Michael had limited visitation with his three children. Jill listened as he talked about how his marriage had always struggled, how his wife had requested time apart while they both evaluated the relationship, and how he grappled with the thought of navigating the future, should they stay apart. His assignments with Jill eventually led to a permanent job with the newspaper, and provided enough extra income for a modest apartment during this separation period.

At first Jill just listened, never sharing the details from her own struggling marriage. But she easily sympathized with Michael's plight. A life partner focused on a career left little time for home, family, and…love.

She was lonely. When she and Rob had first married, he was incredibly attentive. But, over the years, as he pursued opportunities with his flourishing architectural firm, Jill found herself raising kids alone, often covering a plate of leftovers for him to re-heat after late nights at the office.

Michael sensed her loneliness and slowly drew her out of the dark corner where she had resided for so long—as though coaxing an abused puppy from under a house.

Jill felt his caring touch in everything from the brush of his hand on hers when he showed her a photograph, to his reassuring voice. He soothed every offended nerve Rob had left exposed after twenty-six years of placing her at the bottom of his attention-agenda. She had left one dark corner only to find another.

With Michael, life was full of romance, intrigue, and intimacy—all of the things that had gone missing for so long. Gone—like her grown children, the busyness of sports schedules, school, and church—the things that had kept her mind off her loneliness.

With Michael, she had butterflies in her middle again at the anticipation of his smile greeting her every morning at the office. Better than his smile was his kiss. That first kiss had taken them both by surprise. Laughing together over something, he had tugged her arm and pulled her into a warm embrace. As wrong as she knew it was, she melted into his arms. It had been so long since she felt loved. Wanted.

"Hey," Michael's voice interrupted her thoughts.

"*Mmmm?*" Jill squeezed a wedge of lime into her iced water and took a small sip.

"There's something I have to say…" His voice lowered as small beads of perspiration formed at his temples.

Oh no, Jill's mind raced. *He wants me to leave Rob.*

"Wait…" Jill waved her fingers as she held up a hand, scrambling to find words that would let him down gently. Words that wouldn't hurt. She had made up her mind that today it was over. She had to end it.

"No," Michael was firm. "I have to get this out before I lose my nerve."

Jill wondered if he realized her eyes were shut tight.

"Shannon and I are getting back together." Michael's words jumbled out with an exhale. "The time away has made us realize that we want to work things out."

Jill opened her eyes. Had she heard correctly?

Michael's own eyes were fixed on his plate, his food untouched.

"Oh. Well…" Jill realized the circumstances had shifted greatly, but she still struggled to find the right words.

"This time with you has been great." He smiled. "The distraction's been great for both of us. I know things haven't been good for you at home, either." He picked up his fork, playing with the rice on his plate.

Distraction? Jill was indignant. Didn't he care about her? He had certainly acted like it for the past seven months—months of stolen, secret, and sinful moments.

"Yeah," she whispered. "It's been great." Suddenly, there was plenty to say, but the words stuck in her throat. Taking another sip of water, she waved to the server to bring the bill.

ဆ

The crunch of pea gravel in the driveway announced Rob's arrival, and Jill scurried to the kitchen to find something that could pass as dinner. Not hungry herself, she had spent the afternoon in an overstuffed chair near the window, hoping the beautiful view would somehow inspire the right words for the crucial conversation that would need to take place when the door opened.

Rob didn't look like a man with an unfaithful wife. His clean-shaven face looked content and peaceful. No lines of stress could be found around his eyes, no gray at the temples of his thick, chestnut hair. The soft kiss he left on Jill's cheek, as he walked to the counter where she diced a Roma tomato for a salad, felt like the same kiss he had been planting on that cheek for twenty-six years. If anything, Rob seemed happier than he'd ever been.

Setting the serrated knife down, she leaned into the kiss. "Hi, how was your day?" *And, oh, by the way, I've spent the better half of this year cheating on you.*

How did you tell your husband you were having an affair?

"Busy, but I had time for lunch with a client I've been trying to win over for the past month." Rob smiled as he popped a cucumber slice into his mouth and grabbed a plate from the cupboard. "He finally agreed to look at my plans, and it didn't even take Araceli's famous margaritas to convince him!" Rob chuckled as he heaped salad onto his plate and filled a glass with water.

Araceli's? Jill's throat went dry. She was sure she had escaped without being seen, spotted…*caught*. But Rob just said he was there. Having lunch…

There was no handbook on how to confess to an affair. No rules, no instructions, no lessons from Mom on this one. And she couldn't really seek advice from friends.

She touched his shoulder before he sat at the small kitchen table. "Rob, we really need to talk. I'm not quite sure how to say this, but—"

"I almost forgot!" Rob reached for the laptop bag sitting at his feet. Grinning, he pulled out an envelope. "How does a weekend in San Francisco sound?"

"Rob, I don't…I really need to tell you something." Fighting hot tears, Jill knew the words hanging at the back of her throat would change everything.

Rob stood, his hazel eyes meeting her blue ones, holding her gaze. "I know," he said softly. "I *know*." His eyes told her exactly what he knew.

"I guess you saw me today." Tears began to stream down her cheeks, as she lowered her head in shame.

"I've always known."

She couldn't bring herself to ask how. She didn't want to believe that things had changed that much in such a short time. Somehow, it felt safer to believe that things had been wrong for much longer than seven months.

"I have no right to ask," Jill whispered, "but even if you and I are done, can you *ever* forgive me?" Jill shook her head, certain of his answer.

Rob pulled her toward him, smoothing her hair with his warm hand. "I already have."

The dam of reserved tears broke, and Jill fell against her husband's chest. How could this man who worked so hard for twenty-six years, who kept his marriage vows…this man, who didn't deserve to be treated like this, *forgive her*? "How can you be this good…this kind?" Jill asked between sobs.

"Because God forgave me," Rob said simply as if there were no other explanation. "I've turned my back on Him. I've been unfaithful to Him, but He never stopped loving me. I've broken His heart, but He still forgave me. How can I not do the same for the woman I promised to love for the rest of my life?"

There was work to do. It would require a lot of healing and tremendous recovery. But Jill also knew that her husband had chosen to model a divine love that she would never again squander.

Faithful. That's what he was.

Love. That's what *He* is.

In addition to serving in several leadership roles, Lori Hartin writes and speaks for both local and national organizations. An ordained minister, Lori founded Ladybug Women's Ministries to encourage, equip, and empower women everywhere. Learn more at www. LadybugMinistries.org

CROSSING OVER JORDAN
Edward L. Wright

When this wearisome life has ended,

When all is said and done,

As I cross the River Jordan,

Gazing near and far beyond,

I can see my Savior Jesus,

Gloriously seated on His throne.

He softly whispers to me, for I am not alone.

He extends his arms to greet me.

It's incredible what the eyes can see.

He embraces me ever so gently, as I'm snuggled in His arms.

I'm eternally resting within Him; sheltered from all alarms.

I'm comforted by His mercy, with peace surrounding me.

No more pain and agony; I'm content as I can be.

His love is unsurpassed, that overfills my soul.

His precepts are everlasting, as His truth and love unfolds.

EDWARD L. WRIGHT

Born in Tucson, Arizona, Dr. Edward L. Wright spent most of his early years in Denver, Colorado. He is the youngest of eight siblings. As a child, he always enjoyed reading various literary authors such as James Baldwin, Richard Wright, Gwendolyn Brooks, and Countee Cullen.

THE DEER

Elaine C. Juliusson

Maryanne opened her eyes, willing the sun to go away for just a few more minutes, but the intense rays continued to penetrate through the window. She hadn't slept well all night, tossing and turning and regretting last night's quarrel with Robert. It wasn't the first fight they had had in forty years, and probably not the last. But this one left a deeper ache, maybe because it had been so foolish.

She looked at the empty pillow on the other side of the bed. Robert was already up. She longed to cuddle up to him and apologize.

She went into the kitchen instead. No coffee. After so many years of marriage, that told her he was still angry. She found him in the living room, staring at wall.

"British Khaki," he said, continuing the argument from last night.

"Southwest Sunrise," she responded. Last night's argument over the color to paint the living room wall came back in vivid detail. She had finally put her foot down, "It has to be Southwest Sunrise. I'm tired of beige."

He held on to his view. "British Khaki. It's not beige, it's, well, it's khaki!"

Shaking her head, she insisted, "Southwest Sunrise! Are you going to the paint store, or should I? It's nearly closing time."

"I'll go." He grumbled.

He came home with British Khaki. They had argued from dinner through the nightly news, and then went to bed angry.

They both knew better. After so many years, they knew Ephesians 4:26 by heart, "In your anger, do not sin. Do not let the sun go down while you are still angry." One of them had to make an overture of peace.

Now, in the light of morning, she watched him open the can of British Khaki, wishing he had brought home Southwest Sunrise instead. Wouldn't he rather have her happy? *Stubborn old man.* Why was it so hard for him to back down?

Old Blue whined, and Maryanne let him out the door, nearly forgetting about the old dog's needs. She went into the kitchen to make coffee.

Old Blue waddled to the side yard and began a cacophony of wild barking.

Robert stood up from his kneeling position on the floor. "Better go see," he mumbled.

Maryanne joined him. There, tangled in the grape vines was a dead deer.

"A dead deer? What do we do with a dead deer?" Robert mused. "Bury it?"

"We can't dig a hole big enough to bury it," Maryanne said. "I'm calling Jean. She'll know what to do."

Their neighbors, Jean and Joe, had been a wealth of information for Robert and Maryanne since they had moved from their cozy suburban home onto this five-acre ranch.

Maryanne and Robert were the image of *City Slickers*. Maryanne had Jean on the phone, "We have a dead deer in the back yard. What should we do?"

"A deer? That's never happened to us." Jean paused, "Maybe a mountain lion got it. You'll have one tonight, for sure, if you leave it out there."

Maryanne had visions of her, Robert, and Old Blue, defending their ranch from a mountain lion. "Any suggestions?"

"Call the County. They pick up deer on the road."

"Thanks Jean!" Maryanne closed the phone call.

Robert, now on the ladder, suggested, "We can call Sissy and Randy and have them help us."

"No way! One look, and the kids will confirm all their worries about us on this ranch. They'll have us packed and planted in Lincoln Hills Senior Living before you can say 'dead deer.'" She paused for a moment. "I'll google *dead deer in the backyard*." Maryanne found County Wild Animal Removal and punched option one—Dead Deer in the Backyard.

The recorded voice advised, "The County removes dead animals on county roads and public streets. We do not remove animals from backyards. If the home owner can get the carcass to the street, we will pick it up."

"We need to drag it to the road," Maryanne informed Robert, grateful for the diversion from their argument.

"How are we supposed we do that? We're old."

"We have a golf cart. We can load the deer into the bed, drive to the road and dump it out. It'll be easy!" Maryanne looked forward to the adventure. The paint could wait. She went for the golf cart.

"Did you bring a rope?" Robert asked when she drove the cart into the backyard.

"Why?"

He nodded to the deer, which now looked bigger than it had looked before. "It's heavy. I can hardly budge it. We'll have to use the cart to drag it to the road."

After retrieving a rope, they wrapped it around the deer's back legs and gave a good tug to see if it would move. Nothing. They tied the deer to the golf cart and pulled the rope taunt. Dragging it to the road wouldn't be as easy as they first thought.

Maryanne slid behind the steering wheel, "Ready?"

"Stick to the grass, so you don't skin the deer hide on the driveway. When we get to the gate, I'll check the road for traffic. If it's clear, you can drive onto the road, and we'll untie the deer in the ditch." In spite of his apprehension, Robert seemed to be enjoying the adventure.

"Sounds like a plan!" Maryanne started the engine. With a bump, they were off.

Robert jogged behind the cart, staying on the driveway, avoiding mud.

Old Blue was having a field day: a cart, a deer, and a jogging man, all at one time. She was ecstatic.

Maryanne moved quickly over the leaf piles, the fallen branches, and long spring grass, all the way to the gate.

Robert stepped onto the road and gave the all-clear signal.

Maryanne drove onto the edge of the road, close to the ditch.

"Go a little further," Robert called. "You don't want to be in front of the driveway."

Maryanne inched further along the ditch.

Old Blue decided this was a holiday and didn't stay behind the fence. She dashed into the road. A UPS truck screeched to a stop to avoid hitting her, as two cars flew past on the opposite side.

Maryanne panicked and pulled Old Blue into the cart, holding her tight to keep her from dashing back into the road.

The UPS truck rolled past, and Robert untied the deer, giving the signal to go. Maryanne saw a car approaching at the nearby cross road. *I can make a quick U-turn and get back to the driveway.* With one hand on the steering wheel and the other on Old Blue's collar, she forgot that Old Blue was terrified of riding in the golf cart. She turned the wheel sharply and gunned the engine, but the car was coming faster than she thought.

Old Blue tried to jump out, stumbled and landed on her foot on the gas pedal. The cart lurched forward, caught the mud with its front right tire, skidded, and twisted toward Robert.

Maryanne screamed, "Get out of the way!"

Old Blue barked and pulled away from Maryanne.

Robert turned toward the golf cart, his face twisted with shock. On impact, he was thrown back. Maryanne was thrown to the left, and Old Blue to the right. They all landed in the mud next to the dead deer.

The woman in the speeding car stopped, rolled down her window, and called, "Are you hurt? Do you need help?"

Robert waved her on, and then wrapped his mud-covered arms around Maryanne. "I was so scared you were hurt," he breathed into her ear.

"I was sure I killed you!" Maryanne choked back a sob. "I love you so much."

"I love you, too." Robert planted a kiss on her muddy lips.

Old Blue whined and tried to crawl into their embrace.

"Yuck. She's muddy!" Maryanne pushed Old Blue off as she and Robert helped each other up.

"Golf cart's stuck in the mud," Robert said as he tried to push it free. "What do think we should do, now?"

"Let's call Sissy and Randy. I guess we can let them help us get it out of the mud." Maryanne smiled up at Robert. Hand in hand, they walked back toward the house.

"I know. We could paint one wall British Khaki and one Southwest Sunrise!" Maryanne looked happily up at Robert.

He laughed. Releasing her hand, he pulled her close. "Maryanne, that would never work. But, I love you for suggesting it." And then he kissed the tip of her nose.

Elaine Juliusson is a writer. She has two daughters, a son in-law, and a grandson. She lives on a ranch with critters that worm their way into her stories. She has worked as an Analyst, Teacher, Counselor, Bookkeeper, and Expert Witness. She holds an MA in Counseling, and BA in Education.

DYING DAILY FOR LOVE'S SAKE

Sandra Fischer

Poets, philosophers, saints, and greeting card writers have all given us their definitions of love, but all their words and considerations pale before the one given us by the Author of love Himself: *This is how we know what love is: Jesus Christ laid down his life for us. And we ought to lay down our lives for our brothers.* (1 John 3:16)

At first glance, it appears that only by the physical act of dying can we show what real love is. And it's true that many have followed in Christ's footsteps by giving their mortal bodies on behalf of others. Throughout history many Christians have died for their faith or to save others from death. One of the most poignant examples in recent times was the heroic sacrifice of those on Flight 93 on September 11, 2001. A few courageous men stormed the cockpit to prevent the terrorists from using that plane as a "missile" to destroy yet another planned target. By so doing, these men gave their lives and the lives of those on board to spare countless others.

Lisa Beamer's husband, Todd, was one of those heroic men. She was interviewed many times regarding her husband's selfless act. She was asked if he had ever shown by his life to be that kind of hero or if he had performed any similar acts of heroism before this ultimate one in which he gave his life. Lisa Beamer described her husband as an ordinary man who loved God, his family and friends. She said that *everything* he did before 9/11 was preparing him for that day. He hadn't suddenly decided he would become a hero; he had been developing the character of a hero all along by making small, simple everyday sacrifices for the benefit of others. While the act of 9/11 catapulted him into making the ultimate sacrifice, he was already a hero by the way he lived his daily life.

Few of us will be called to die as Todd Beamer and others have, but we are called to lay down our lives each day by dying to our own selfish desires in "little sacrifices" to illustrate the principle of love shown by our Lord. What we may consider to be small considerations are really revelations of our hearts. We can find them given in Scripture. And, we can see them expressed daily in infinitesimal ways, such as:

Forgiving someone who has slighted you in word or deed.

> *Forgiving one another as Christ forgave you.* (Colossians 3:13)

Listening to someone to sincerely try to understand.

> *A fool has no delight in understanding, but in expressing his own heart.* (Proverbs 18:2)

Letting someone in line ahead of you when it's really your turn.

> *Honor one another above yourselves.* (Romans 12:10b)

Smiling at the fast food server and thanking her, even when she's not so fast.

Be kind and compassionate to one another...
(Ephesians 4:32)

Minding what you say rather than saying what's on your mind.

...and we take captive every thought to make it obedient to Christ. (2 Corinthians 10:5b)

Not insisting on your way as the only way.

Do not think of yourself more highly than you ought— (Romans 12:3b)

Showing mercy and leaving justice to God.

Do not take revenge...leave room for God's wrath. (Romans 12:19a)

Saying "thank you" and "I love you" often.

In everything give thanks... (2 Thessalonians 5:18a)

Love one another for love is from God... (1 John 4:7b)

Saying "I'm sorry" whenever necessary.

Clothe yourself with humility toward one another... (1 Peter 3:5b)

These examples of everyday gestures represent the giving of ourselves in a myriad of ways. This is dying daily for love's sake. Jesus said that there is no greater love than laying down our lives for our friends, not necessarily all at once, but by each day choosing to surrender in obedience to His commands and His example. Every day we have opportunities to show kindness instead of criticism, mercy instead of judgment, grace instead of condemnation, and forbearance instead of intolerance.

The Lord did such small acts every day on His way to the cross. If we are to truly follow Him as He has called us to do, we can do no less. When He commanded followers to take up their cross in Luke 9:23, He said, *Whoever wants to be my disciple must deny themselves and take up their cross daily and follow me.* By using the word *daily*, He was showing how self-sacrificial love is not a one time, all-in event, but a constant giving of ourselves. He told us how to love, He showed us how to love, and each word, each deed was with our benefit in mind, not His. He loved by dying daily to self, showing us how we should live, a mysterious paradox—by laying down our lives daily for others we show the amazing love of Christ.

Sandra Fischer taught high school English and owned a Christian bookstore in Indiana before retiring and devoting time to writing. Many of her stories and articles are gleaned from her experiences growing up in the Midwest. She is the author of the book, **Seasons in the Garden.**

My Greatest Adventure

Jasmine Schmidt

It only took one glance,

To set my heart in motion.

It only took a second smile,

To steal my heart completely.

You have a hold so tender,

Breaking down my walls.

You have a way with words,

Sending warmth into my soul.

Through the tides of time,

You are forever constant.

You reassure me with truth,

And wash away my fears.

You tell me that you love me,

As if there were no tomorrow.

You place stars in my sky,

And bring sun into my world.

With every day that passes,

I fall in love again.

My greatest adventure,

Is a life loved with you.

Jasmine Schmidt is a children's and YA fiction writer as well as a poet. Writing is her passion and her calling. God gave her a talent with words and she writes to bring Him glory. Jasmine's goal is to provide readers with clean, intriguing books and emotionally moving poems to enjoy.

What Manner of Love

Tessa Burns

Behold what manner of love the Father has bestowed on us, that we should be called the children of God. (1 John 3:1 NKJV)

I have always loved this verse. Gratitude rises from my heart at the thought. The Creator of all the universe gently reached down, held me in His hands, and said, "You are Mine." What a privilege, and yet how difficult to fathom that a Holy God would be willing to call Himself my Father, and call me His child. Oh, how great a love!

How could a perfect God remotely interact with a fallen individual like myself? Like any of us? I often feel that I must earn this love in some way, or do penance simply because I am human. How can God look my way, or even be aware of little-ol'-me?

But God…Oh, what an amazing statement…But God…

But God demonstrates His own love toward us, in that while we were still sinners, Christ died for us. (Romans 5:8 NKJV)

But God…knew humankind would sin given free choice. But God…still wanted a relationship with fallen man. But God… knew we wouldn't be able to bridge the gap between us on our own; He knew He alone was able to devise and execute a plan to redeem man back to Himself.

For God so loved the world that He gave His only begotten Son, that whoever believes in Him should not perish but have everlasting life. (John 3:16 NKJV)

For when we were still sinners without strength, in due time Christ died for the ungodly. (Romans 5:6 NKJV)

I do not have the strength within myself to make things right, but for whatever reason there seems to be an innate desire to try and fix it myself. I can't. Not on my own. None of us can. The only fix is the love of God that pulls us up out of the ashes and calls us His own. Only the shed blood of Jesus that brings us to life from the dead can correct our fallenness. This is love: the willingness to be spit at, mocked, even crucified for the joy set before Him. Christ endured all of this with the vision of each of us saved by His righteous act. The price that only He could pay.

You know, God could have looked at us from His Holy habitation and said, "What a mess! Forget this! Forget them!" and turned His face away. But He didn't. He sent Jesus, and Jesus said, "Here I am, send Me," knowing full well what He would have to endure. But He could see me, He could see you, and He said, "I will go. For them. They are My inheritance; they are Mine. I will not turn away from them, I will not leave them as orphans; I will not abandon them. I will go to them. I will lay down My life for them, because I love them."

In our weakness, Christ showed Himself strong. It is the deepest, most ancient magic of all—the power of the cross, the power of the resurrection, the power of love.

Tessa lives in Northern California with her husband and three grown children. Her hope, as she journeys through life, is to encourage others to notice the beauty all around them and inside of them, and to understand and know how deeply they are loved.

No Loving Men

Tessa Bertoldi

"No loving men left" is a complaint I frequently hear from unhappy women. It seems to be more of a side order of husband bashing, frequently followed by another divorce announcement. Television programs often highlight how dissatisfied women are with a lack of good, loving men. If you listen to popular talk, you could assume loving men are as extinct as a *T. rex*.

Don't get me wrong, my marriage was not perfect. My beloved could not walk on water. Unless of course, he believed that Jesus told him to get out of the boat and start walking. Then amazing things would happen. I've been a widow for five years. I knew I was fortunate while my beloved was still living, but now I understand it goes beyond fortunate firmly into blessed.

So where have loving men gone, are they really gone? I asked the Lord to remind me of men who act out their love for His creations. It's surprising how we overlook things that are right in front of us. Here is a sample of the loving men in my life.

My handyman is Dave, he never really accepted his divorce. Mr. and Mrs. Dave were caught up in the daily business of work and raising children, three boys and a beautiful girl. I first got to know Dave years ago, and he shared with me that he wasn't the same person when married to Mrs. Dave. He was busy providing for his family and didn't always express his love in ways she understood. He admitted he was often frustrated, harsh, and angry. He didn't love his wife and children any less. The anger and frustration between the couple rose to a level Mrs. Dave no longer wanted to live with. She gave the missus part back, and Dave was devastated. He never gave up hope that they would be happy again. Dave began to practice being the loving man he thought his family deserved. He began to practice what he believed the church was created for.

Religion that God our Father accepts as pure and faultless is this: to look after orphans and widows in their distress and to keep oneself from being polluted by the world. (James 1:27)

Today, Dave demonstrates his love by taking care of widows and orphans. He repairs plumbing, patches floors and other needed household repairs, most of the time without accepting payment. He has been demonstrating God's love for decades. Things haven't worked out exactly the way Dave wanted, but he is no longer angry and frustrated. Everyone loves to be around him, and children flock to him. He is everyone's favorite grandpa! His relationship with his adult children has improved, and he spends quality time with his grandchildren.

Next, is a family that most would look at and assume it is a good home situation. Distress and crises can be hidden from the world by carefully created self-defense mechanisms and layers of legal protection. The court removed two siblings and gave custody to their aunt. The family patriarch decided that the children should go back to their father, who was already ruled unfit in ways that would make you sick.

New adult Fiero* is the stable person in this family. He has a good job and his own apartment. Taking legal action against his aunt and father could have resulted in the court separating and sending his cousins off to foster homes. He managed to talk his aunt into letting him take his cousins, persuading her that they needed to grow up together to develop a sense of family. Fiero receives no money for raising his cousins. They now eat regularly and come to school in clean clothing, their behavior has improved. Time passed, and Fiero petitioned the court for custody. The family cannot contest his efforts because he is the only family member with citizenship. Names have been changed and records sealed, Fiero risked a lot for his cousins.

Don is extremely qualified, but took a job with a non-profit disaster relief organization. He is paid typical non-profit wages, yet frequently travels to training and disaster sites. The wages paid never compensate him for the hours or the amount of caring he puts into helping others in need. He is passionate about demonstrating God's love when people are at their lowest point. When a fire, mudslide, flood, twister, tornado, or earthquake takes a home, Don mobilizes people, supplies, and money to assist hurting people. Most of the people he provides aid for never even know his name. They still feel the results of his love.

Paul is a minister who never saw the twists and turns his life would take. He married his beautiful, talented wife and had two children. His daughter developed dysautonomia at a young age, a disease difficult to diagnose. It is a dysfunction of the autonomic nervous system. This system controls automatic body functions, including breathing, digestion, and circulation. A dysautonomia patient never knows when it will strike or what will be affected. Paul and his wife grew closer together and God, as others suggested their daughter was suffering from psychosomatic symptoms and insisted she be taken to a psychologist. Child protective services was called by someone who did not understand the disease, causing discomfort and confusion. The family's world got smaller to protect the fragile daughter and the family unit. Paul adjusted his schedule and employment to be more available. There is no cure, only treatment for the symptoms and an early death, usually in pre-teens. Her longevity has required heroic efforts by her parents and only sibling. Paul continues to intercede with the Heavenly Father for his daughter's health. Her attitude reflects the love of her family, she continues to be positive and does not fear death. Death is anticipated as a welcome release for her, but she prays that God will take her when the time is right for her parents.

Greater love has no one than this: to lay down one's life for one's friends. (John 15:13)

The last time I saw this beautiful soul, she was twenty-two and still able to communicate with me. Her quiet confidence and love for God humbled me then and continues now. She cares more for the people around her after she will be gone. The love demonstrated by her father does not stop there. When my beloved passed away, Paul was there for me. We do not even go to the same church, we share the same Savior. Paul understands the pain of death and separation from our loved ones. He has already experienced it and lives with its shadow daily. He makes time to help others, assists the deaf community, and demonstrates love. He organizes help and training on large and small scales and is skilled in listening and coaching. I don't expect him to ever stop being who God designed him to be.

Then there is my beloved. His foster sister was my best friend. He knew my abusive ex-husband from a distance. I found myself a single mother, on my own, with limited money and technology resources. My friend suggested I call her engineer brother. He immediately drove an hour to my home, removed my hard drive, whacked it with a hammer, and mounted it upside down. He left instructions to download data and to keep the computer on, he would be back with a new hard drive. He refused money, so I thanked him with a meal. Years later, our friendship developed into love, and we were married. I was blessed to be able to watch his loving acts of service for fifteen more years. Repairing a college student's computer right before a midnight deadline. Rescuing two teenage boys living on the street and bringing them home to me. Holding a child lashing out with her fists, angry at her abusive, negligent father. My beloved held her as she beat him and calmly told her he loved her. He got up early in winter to turn on heat so the senior ladies' Bible study would be comfortable. He drove to the pregnancy center (because God told him to) with a check for $2,000, exactly the amount of rent they were praying for to keep the doors open. He was raised with next to nothing, often starving, so no one ever left his presence or home hungry. I continue to honor his memory by always making sure no one leaves my home hungry.

There are loving men all around us if we choose to see. They crave our respect and need just as much love as anyone. There are many more examples, but this anthology has a word limit. By the way, T Rex is alive and well too, he has evolved into our modern-day poultry.

*names changed

Tessa Bertoldi

Tessa Bertoldi, a secret writer through school and years as a Risk Manager, a mom and Technical Writer. Set free, her current efforts include a post-apocalyptic sci-fi novel, work with the National Novel Writing Month and Staff Volunteer for the San Francisco Writer's Conference. Her next life chapters promise to be even more exciting.

Abandoned, But Wanted

Jean Johnson

Although my father and my mother have abandoned me,
yet the Lord will take me up [adopt me as His child].

(Psalms 27:10 AMPC)

After my mother abandoned me when I was four years old, I waited daily by my bedroom window for her. Surely, she made a mistake and realizes the man she's with is evil. She will come back to me.

Every day for a year, I waited with great yearning for her, hoping she wanted me.

On my fifth birthday, I sat by the window a bit longer with streaming tears. *Momma, oh momma, I miss you so much!* My tiny heart ached with incredible loss. Something churned within me, and a final truth jolted my five-year-old mind. I wasn't the boy she had hoped for. *She's not coming back for me. She doesn't love me. That's okay. I don't need a mother!* Oh, how I sobbed.

This was a five year old's little vow, born out of intense pain. What did I know?

God has knit each of us together in such a way that we need our mother and father. It has taken me most of my life to heal from this ragged hole in my heart. And to intimately know the true eternal love of Abba, our wonderful father, God.

~

My Heavenly Vision

As I lay on my bed with my head buried in my quilt, tears continued to flow. My room filled with a penetrating bright light, yet I didn't feel dread or fear. I looked up and saw something so unbelievably beautiful, my tears ceased.

In front of me stood a man radiantly dressed in a blazing white, long robe. His eyes flashed with brilliant and fiery love. His scarred hands stretched toward me.

My young heart leapt in response to this warm love pouring over me. Somehow, I knew this was Jesus, as my blind father described Him.

He approached my bed and said, "My beloved child, come to Me. I will give you My love and peace." Then He reached out and touched my head.

All distress and fear vanished. I felt like I was hugged in His soothing love. Though I had a bleeding child's heart, something changed that day.

~

As an adult peering into my early experience, I see something profound. Jesus revealed Himself to pour His lavish love, peace, and grace over me. This special double grace enabled me to go through a lifetime of hardships without falling apart, or becoming completely overcome by Satan's forces.

I gave my heart to Jesus at age seven and the Holy Spirit at seven and a half. He said we would have many trials and tribulations while here on earth, but we are to be encouraged, because He will walk with us through what we face. Jesus has never left my side, even on the occasions I wanted to end my life.

I know the plans I have for you, says the Lord, they are plans for good and not for evil, to give you a future and a hope. (Jeremiah 29:11)

I am loved with an everlasting love, and fully accepted as His beloved. Nothing can make His love flee from me, not death, nor angels, or demons. I believe Jesus gave me this vision as a child to reveal His love for me. Most importantly, He showed me that I was His adopted and wanted child. To Him be all of the glory and praise forever and ever!

Jean Johnson's avid love of reading and writing throughout her life stemmed from those early childhood years when she read stories to her blind father. In May 2014, Jean graduated with English honors. Currently, she writes short stories, articles, book reviews for her grief group, devotionals, poems, and blogs.

LOVE FROM DUST

Ethan Ruoff

July 3rd, 3056

Half the population had been lost in six years of war. But, under the Treaty of Islands, none of the flying islands could house the military, or be attacked. In Aroul, I felt somewhat safe.

First period Thursday morning, I sat in the back, left corner of history, waiting. Others finally arrived. I recognized a few. Then unfortunately, *he* arrived. He's a really discouraging reminder that pain still lives—even in Aroul. His name is Josh. Every day he chooses one person to torment.

Some have even died.

I flinched when he sat next to me.

"What's up, bro?"

"Your ego." I didn't look at him.

"Ooh, nice comeback, where'd you find it? The black market?"

"Seriously? That wasn't even funny," I said. Fighting him would seal my doom. I stayed quiet. He grew bored of calling me names and left, but I knew he'd return.

The holographic teacher activated and wandered the room. "New students, come forward, introduce yourselves, then we'll look at the War of 2017 in our history tablets. Who will go first?" Ten people stood. One kid spoke up.

"Hello, I'm Flynn. This is my sister, Claire."

Claire glanced around the room. Her gaze met mine for a moment. I didn't hear the rest of the names. Most would probably die soon.

Josh took Flynn's seat. Flynn and Claire exchanged a glance.

"Hey, you guys can sit here." I waved them over.

"Thanks," Flynn said.

Claire's eyes locked with mine. Her face turned pink, and she hesitated a second. She looked down, tugged her dark brown hair, and glanced at me. Her beautiful blue eyes sparkled.

Flynn sat in front of me. Claire sat to my right.

"Th-thank you," she said looking at the floor.

"No problem. Most of my friends left for war, never to return."

They both nodded.

"I think it's the same for all of us," Flynn said.

We got acquainted quickly since we shared all of our classes.

I started liking school.

❧

One morning, a crowd gathered outside. I pushed to the front. Josh pounded Flynn. One of Josh's henchmen held Claire by the arms. She looked at me. Tears fell across her face while she grit her teeth and tried to pull away.

When he paused and stepped back from Flynn, I rammed Josh in the ribs with my elbow, knocking him over. His henchman froze. Claire kicked hard behind her. His grip dropped.

She ran to Flynn and helped him stand up. Blood gushed from his forehead.

"What happened?" I asked.

Claire pointed, "Flynn intervened when Josh pushed a kid. Then Josh threw Qailent dust at Flynn and pushed him to the ground. Please, help me get him to a hospital!"

I caught Flynn as he started to fall and lowered him to the ground. "Get help," I told Claire as we knelt down.

Claire tapped twice on her holograph bracelet, and the school medic appeared. The medic touched Claire and Flynn, and we teleported to the hospital.

დ

"Wait, why am I here?"

"Don't you want to see if your friend survives?" the medic said to me.

I pulled my jacket around me to stop the sudden chill. I couldn't look away from Claire's downcast face while we waited.

She kept glancing at the door. "He was protecting me," she said. "Josh was flirting. I tried to ignore him and walk away. He grabbed me."

"That's when Flynn came?"

"His gang surrounded us. He said he'd kill my brother if I ignored him. Flynn came over and tried to pull me away."

Just then, the medic returned.

"We think he suffered a concussion. He isn't exactly…himself. You can see him now."

I followed Claire.

"Claire?" Flynn tried to sit up.

She ran and hugged him.

The cloth covering his forehead reddened.

She stepped back and Flynn noticed me. "Hey, what's up?"

The cloth continued to redden.

"I want to warn you…I'm fading."

I saw Claire's eyes fill with tears.

Flynn stopped talking.

"I'm just happy you're still here," Claire said. "Josh hit you really hard."

"Well, I'm a…fighter." Flynn looked down. "I'm slipping, aren't I?"

Claire sniffed a little and started to cry. I was on the verge of crying, too.

She leaned her head on my shoulder. When I put my arm around her, a warm feeling passed through me.

Flynn looked up and smiled. "You two would make such a cute couple."

Claire's head shot up, and I moved my arm back to my side and stood straight.

Flynn laughed, the cloth on his forehead reddened more.

"I've seen these things happen—even in our deadly world. You two are perfect for each other."

I stayed silent. I didn't want to make it more awkward.

"Trust me, you will just need to make a move, otherwise her feelings will pass you by." Flynn said.

He shivered, and his eyes rolled back in their sockets.

"Get out!" The medic shouted running back into the room.

We hurried out but listened. Silence hung for several moments. Suddenly we heard, "Clear!" and *bzzz*.

Claire stood in the corner bawling.

In the same instant, I reached my hand toward her and she turned quickly. Her arms wrapped around my neck. She sobbed into my shoulder. I froze and then returned the embrace. Again, I felt warm. "I-it's gonna be okay. He'll get through this." I tried not to cry.

"Thank you for being here. I hate being alone," she said.

At that moment, the medic returned. "He's barely hanging on. Seems he was dosed with Qailent dust. It's killing him. I'm sorry. There is no cure."

Claire ran into the room. I started to follow, but the medic whispered to me, "He only has minutes." I took a breath and entered.

"Flynn!" Claire grabbed his hand.

Flynn looked at us.

"So, how's it going with you two?" One side of his mouth turned up.

"Flynn, you can't just act like this isn't happening!" I told him.

"I know what's happening. I'm not gonna get better. Just another death to add to so many others. I want to know my sister is going to be okay," he whispered. "So, how's it going with you two?"

We both stood still for a second.

"It's…good…" I said.

"Yeah…" Claire said.

Flynn tipped his head, "What do you think of each other?"

I blurted, "She's smart, kind, and beautiful."

Claire smiled. She looked back at me, and our eyes met again. Her face lit up. "You're the nicest guy I've met."

"We use to live out in the country. We didn't meet a lot of other people there." Flynn replied.

"That doesn't change my feelings." She smiled.

Flynn's glance passed between us. Claire and I were still smiling at each other. "Wow. That was easy."

"I need water," Claire said. "Haven't had any all day."

I reached to stop her, but Flynn shook his head.

When she stepped outside, Flynn said, "Listen, I don't have long. I've seen the effects of the Qailent dust. That's how our parents died. This will not end well."

"Your parents are dead?"

Flynn nodded. "I love my sister. I'm all she has. Promise me that you'll take care of her. Even if this whole thing doesn't work out between you, protect her until you find someone else to do it. I trust you more than anyone else. Please don't let me down."

Claire walked in.

Flynn sagged back into the pillow. A machine started beeping.

Closing his eyes, Flynn drew in a shaky breath and the machine flat-lined.

⁂

Suddenly we were teleported back to fifth period just in time to get our homework. Claire sat next to me. Death didn't stop anything anymore.

Claire fought crying.

I reached for her hand. She had a strong grip. I didn't let go.

The bell rang. We walked out together. "I g-gotta go h-home." She wiped tears from her face. She'd been through a lot. She took a step.

"I'll go with you," I said. "I don't want you to be alone. Why don't we walk this time."

"So, you want to walk me home?" The edges of her mouth turned up slightly.

"Uh…yes…well, I mean…uh…" This was all so new. She was the first person I'd ever liked.

"Sure." She half smiled.

We talked the whole way home.

"Thanks for staying with me today."

"Sorry about your brother. The rest has been nice, though—"

She leaned forward, kissed me on the cheek, and walked to her door. The AI assistant opened it for her. "Welcome home, Miss Claire."

Claire turned and looked at me.

I stood awkwardly and touched my cheek. "Uh, th-thanks."

She laughed, slipping inside.

I smiled and touched my holograph watch. Going to school tomorrow looked better than normal.

Glossary:

Aroul—a safe island under the Treaty of Islands

Qailent—poisonous dust with no cure

AI—artificial intelligence robot

Ethan is a middle school student who attends a Christian school in Northern California and loves God greatly. He has a great imagination, and used that to start writing when he was eleven.

What Dad Would Tell the World

Michelle Van Vliet

On July 9, 2015, my father was diagnosed with an aggressive form of leukemia. Six short months later, his fight ended, and my dad found himself in God's love, embraced by Jesus for real and forever. Two weeks before he died, I sat with my dad and asked him: "Dad, if you could tell the world anything, what would it be?"

First, he said, "Following Jesus doesn't always lead us to a place where we want to be." I noticed a Lenten devotional in his Bible that said as much. It seemed God was preparing him before he ever knew he'd be taking this journey.

It's easy to assume if we follow Jesus and do what's "right" it will lead to a "blessing" we expect. At first my dad was angry about cancer and the way it was stealing his life. He felt cheated and so did a lot of us. There were many dark days. Yet, through a disease that was taking my dad's life far sooner than he wanted, he was learning the blessing of following Jesus was actually Jesus, not necessarily good circumstances. And the gift of following Christ was not his *presents* wrapped in neat little bows set pristinely upon a shelf. Rather, His *presence* that comes near when everything else goes dark—when life unravels those pretty bows and bursts out of our tidy boxes.

I suppose that's why he also said to me during the same visit, "Michellie, don't fall too in love with the world. Wear it loosely." Dad began to understand how his despair (and ours) is often rooted in our commitment to the very temporal and unpredictable things of this place called Earth. We strain after our dreams and demand our rights. We spend time climbing the corporate ladder and dusting off old trophies.

But loosening his grip on those things allowed my dad to surrender himself to the story God was writing. He encountered God in that surrender even when the journey did not lead to a place he wanted to be. In the struggle, he found the blessings and goodness of God. It showed up in the presence of friends who stayed by him as he weathered the last few months. It sometimes appeared in the night as God brought heavenly hosts to hover and attend him in his fear. It showed up in caregivers who gently came alongside to comfort his pain. It showed up in strained relationships now made whole. That was a big deal to him.

That day, my dad talked about those relationships. He said, "I wouldn't let lousy relationships go unattended. I wouldn't put off conflict. I would have been less angry. I would pick relationships over everything else and I would do it more."

I asked what *everything else* was and he said, "My rights, my expectations, my ideals, my pride. There is never a conflict so big that it should eclipse the relationship or our ability to love in it. Never."

My dad didn't say this because he always got it right. He said it because he often did the heart work when he got it wrong.

As I consider the eternal home my dad now enjoys, perhaps if he could say anything to us now, he'd tell us how complete and beautiful it is—that what seems incomplete to us now here on Earth, is already made whole in eternity. He'd say God's promises are all true, every one of them. He'd tell us God is gloriously good, and how he is at home in His love—a love that is every bit and even more than we've imagined. He'd invite us to taste it, to trust the journey and to know that even when it takes us down paths we'd rather not travel, chances are it's in those dark places where we will find God in the way we've always longed to know Him.

Michelle Van Vliet is a pastor's wife, writer, and speaker residing in Turlock, California. As a graduate of the Renovaré Institute of Christian Spiritual Formation, her honest and energetic approach offers a fresh perspective of discipleship that moves beyond living for Jesus to envisioning a life of joyful companionship with Him.

Inspire Press is a division of

Inspire Christian Writers

Inspire Christian Writers provides a network of support, encouragement, education, and spiritual growth for Christian writers. We minister biblical truths with excellence, clarity, and love, to transform lives and the publishing industry. To learn more and/or join, please visit **inspirewriters.com**

Also available from Inspire Press
Inspire Trust, 2012
Inspire Faith, 2013
Friends of Inspire Faith, 2013
Inspired Glimpses of God's Presence, 2013
Inspire Victory, 2014
Inspire Promise, 2014
Exit Cyrus, 2014
DogSpirations, 2015
How to Love God with All Your Heart, 2015
Inspire Forgiveness, 2015
The Never Ending Gifts, 2016
Inspire Joy, 2016

Coming Fall 2017 from Inspire Press

Inspire Kindness

To receive submission guidelines and/or publication information, please email **inspirepress@inspirewriters.com**